CONTENTS

1.INTERACTIVE ELEMENTS

Image Slider

```
<!DOCTYPE html>
<html lang="en">
<head>
  <meta charset="UTF-8">
  <meta name="viewport" content="width=device-width, initial-scale=1.0">
  <title>Image Slider</title>
  <style>
    body { font-family: Arial, sans-serif; text-align: center; }
    .slider { position: relative; width: 80%; max-width: 800px; margin: auto; overflow: hidden; }
    .slides { display: flex; transition: transform 0.5s ease-in-out; }
    .slides img { width: 100%; border-radius: 10px; }
    .navigation { position: absolute; top: 50%; width: 100%; display: flex; justify-content: space-between; transform: translateY(-50%); }
    .prev, .next { background-color: rgba(0, 0, 0, 0.5); color: white; padding: 10px; border: none; cursor: pointer; border-radius: 50%; }
  </style>
</head>
<body>
  <h1>Image Slider</h1>
  <div class="slider">
    <div class="slides">
      <img src="https://via.placeholder.com/800x400/ff7f7f/333333?text=Image+1" alt="Image 1">
      <img src="https://via.placeholder.com/800x400/7fbfff/333333?text=Image+2" alt="Image 2">
      <img src="https://via.placeholder.com/800x400/7fff7f/333333?text=Image+3" alt="Image 3">
    </div>
```

```
    <div class="navigation">
      <button class="prev" onclick="prevSlide()">□ </button>
      <button class="next" onclick="nextSlide()">□ </button>
    </div>
  </div>
  <script>
    let currentIndex = 0;
    const slides = document.querySelector('.slides');
    const totalSlides = document.querySelectorAll('.slides img').length;
    function showSlide(index) {
      if (index >= totalSlides) {
        currentIndex = 0;
      } else if (index < 0) {
        currentIndex = totalSlides - 1;
      } else {
        currentIndex = index;
      }
      const offset = -currentIndex * 100;
      slides.style.transform = `translateX(${offset}%)`;
    }
    function nextSlide() {
      showSlide(currentIndex + 1);
    }
    function prevSlide() {
      showSlide(currentIndex - 1);
    }
    setInterval(nextSlide, 3000); // Change image every 3 seconds
  </script>
</body>
</html>
```

Lightbox for Images

```
<!DOCTYPE html>
<html lang="en">
<head>
  <meta charset="UTF-8">
  <meta name="viewport" content="width=device-width, initial-scale=1.0">
  <title>Lightbox for Images</title>
  <style>
    body { font-family: Arial, sans-serif; text-align: center; }
    .gallery img { width: 200px; cursor: pointer; margin: 10px; border-radius: 10px; }
    .lightbox { display: none; position: fixed; top: 0; left: 0; width: 100%; height: 100%;
background: rgba(0, 0, 0, 0.8); justify-content: center; align-items: center; }
    .lightbox img { max-width: 90%; max-height: 90%; }
    .lightbox:target { display: flex; }
    .close { position: absolute; top: 20px; right: 20px; color: white; font-size: 24px; text-
decoration: none; }
  </style>
</head>
<body>
  <h1>Lightbox for Images</h1>
  <div class="gallery">
    <a href="#img1"><img
src="https://via.placeholder.com/600x400/ff7f7f/333333?text=Image+1" alt="Image 1"></a>
    <a href="#img2"><img
src="https://via.placeholder.com/600x400/7fbfff/333333?text=Image+2" alt="Image 2"></a>
    <a href="#img3"><img
src="https://via.placeholder.com/600x400/7fff7f/333333?text=Image+3" alt="Image 3"></a>
  </div>
  <div id="img1" class="lightbox">
    <a href="#" class="close">&times;</a>
```

```
    <img src="https://via.placeholder.com/600x400/ff7f7f/333333?text=Image+1" alt="Image 1">
  </div>
  <div id="img2" class="lightbox">
    <a href="#" class="close">&times;</a>
    <img src="https://via.placeholder.com/600x400/7fbfff/333333?text=Image+2" alt="Image 2">
  </div>
  <div id="img3" class="lightbox">
    <a href="#" class="close">&times;</a>
    <img src="https://via.placeholder.com/600x400/7fff7f/333333?text=Image+3" alt="Image 3">
  </div>
</body>
</html>
```

Accordions

```
<!DOCTYPE html>
<html lang="en">
<head>
  <meta charset="UTF-8">
  <meta name="viewport" content="width=device-width, initial-scale=1.0">
  <title>Accordions</title>
  <style>
    body { font-family: Arial, sans-serif; }
    .accordion { margin: 10px 0; }
    .accordion-header { cursor: pointer; background: lightgray; padding: 10px; border: 1px solid #ccc; }
    .accordion-content { display: none; padding: 10px; border: 1px solid #ccc; border-top: none; }
    .accordion-content.show { display: block; }
  </style>
</head>
<body>
  <h1>Accordions</h1>
```

```
  <div class="accordion">
    <div class="accordion-header" onclick="toggleAccordion(this)">Section 1</div>
    <div class="accordion-content">
      <p>This is the content of section 1.</p>
    </div>
  </div>
  <div class="accordion">
    <div class="accordion-header" onclick="toggleAccordion(this)">Section 2</div>
    <div class="accordion-content">
      <p>This is the content of section 2.</p>
    </div>
  </div>
  <div class="accordion">
    <div class="accordion-header" onclick="toggleAccordion(this)">Section 3</div>
    <div class="accordion-content">
      <p>This is the content of section 3.</p>
    </div>
  </div>
  <script>
    function toggleAccordion(header) {
      const content = header.nextElementSibling;
      content.classList.toggle('show');
    }
  </script>
</body>
</html>
```

Tabs

```
<!DOCTYPE html>
<html lang="en">
```

```
<head>
  <meta charset="UTF-8">
  <meta name="viewport" content="width=device-width, initial-scale=1.0">
  <title>Tabs</title>
  <style>
    body { font-family: Arial, sans-serif; }
    .tab { cursor: pointer; padding: 10px 20px; display: inline-block; background: lightgray;
margin-right: 2px; }
    .tab-content { display: none; padding: 20px; border: 1px solid #ccc; border-top: none; }
    .tab-content.active { display: block; }
  </style>
</head>
<body>
  <h1>Tabs</h1>
  <div id="tab1" class="tab" onclick="showTab('tab1')">Tab 1</div>
  <div id="tab2" class="tab" onclick="showTab('tab2')">Tab 2</div>
  <div id="tab3" class="tab" onclick="showTab('tab3')">Tab 3</div>
  <div id="tab1Content" class="tab-content">
    <h2>Content 1</h2>
    <p>This is the content of tab 1.</p>
  </div>
  <div id="tab2Content" class="tab-content">
    <h2>Content 2</h2>
    <p>This is the content of tab 2.</p>
  </div>
  <div id="tab3Content" class="tab-content">
    <h2>Content 3</h2>
    <p>This is the content of tab 3.</p>
  </div>
```

```
  <script>
    function showTab(tabId) {
      const contents = document.querySelectorAll('.tab-content');
      contents.forEach(content => content.classList.remove('active'));
      document.getElementById(tabId + 'Content').classList.add('active');
    }
  </script>
</body>
</html>
```

Tooltips

```
<!DOCTYPE html>
<html lang="en">
<head>
  <meta charset="UTF-8">
  <meta name="viewport" content="width=device-width, initial-scale=1.0">
  <title>Tooltips</title>
  <style>
    body { font-family: Arial, sans-serif; }
    .tooltip { position: relative; display: inline-block; cursor: pointer; }
    .tooltip .tooltiptext { visibility: hidden; width: 120px; background-color: black; color: #fff; text-align: center; border-radius: 5px; padding: 5px; position: absolute; z-index: 1; bottom: 125%; left: 50%; margin-left: -60px; opacity: 0; transition: opacity 0.3s; }
    .tooltip:hover .tooltiptext { visibility: visible; opacity: 1; }
  </style>
</head>
<body>
  <h1>Tooltips</h1>
  <p>Hover over the text below to see the tooltip:</p>
  <div class="tooltip">Hover me
    <div class="tooltiptext">Tooltip text</div>
```

```
  </div>
</body>
</html>
```

Dropdowns

```
<!DOCTYPE html>
<html lang="en">
<head>
  <meta charset="UTF-8">
  <meta name="viewport" content="width=device-width, initial-scale=1.0">
  <title>Dropdowns</title>
  <style>
    body { font-family: Arial, sans-serif; }
    .dropdown { position: relative; display: inline-block; }
    .dropdown-content { display: none; position: absolute; background-color: #f9f9f9; box-shadow: 0px 8px 16px 0px rgba(0,0,0,0.2); z-index: 1; }
    .dropdown-content a { color: black; padding: 12px 16px; text-decoration: none; display: block; }
    .dropdown-content a:hover { background-color: #f1f1f1; }
    .dropdown:hover .dropdown-content { display: block; }
  </style>
</head>
<body>
  <h1>Dropdowns</h1>
  <div class="dropdown">
    <button>Dropdown</button>
    <div class="dropdown-content">
      <a href="#">Link 1</a>
      <a href="#">Link 2</a>
      <a href="#">Link 3</a>
    </div>
```

```
  </div>
</body>
</html>
```

Drag and Drop

```
<!DOCTYPE html>
<html lang="en">
<head>
  <meta charset="UTF-8">
  <meta name="viewport" content="width=device-width, initial-scale=1.0">
  <title>Drag and Drop</title>
  <style>
    body { font-family: Arial, sans-serif; }
    .draggable { width: 100px; height: 100px; background-color: #ff7f7f; margin: 10px; display:
inline-block; cursor: move; }
    .dropzone { width: 300px; height: 300px; border: 2px dashed #ccc; display: inline-block;
vertical-align: top; }
  </style>
</head>
<body>
  <h1>Drag and Drop</h1>
  <div class="draggable" draggable="true" ondragstart="drag(event)" id="drag1"></div>
  <div class="dropzone" ondrop="drop(event)" ondragover="allowDrop(event)"></div>
  <script>
    function allowDrop(event) {
      event.preventDefault();
    }

    function drag(event) {
      event.dataTransfer.setData("text", event.target.id);
    }
```

```
    function drop(event) {
      event.preventDefault();
      const data = event.dataTransfer.getData("text");
      event.target.appendChild(document.getElementById(data));
    }
  </script>
</body>
</html>
```

Image Gallery with Filters

```
<!DOCTYPE html>
<html lang="en">
<head>
  <meta charset="UTF-8">
  <meta name="viewport" content="width=device-width, initial-scale=1.0">
  <title>Image Gallery with Filters</title>
  <style>
    body { font-family: Arial, sans-serif; }
    .gallery { display: flex; flex-wrap: wrap; }
    .gallery img { width: 200px; margin: 10px; display: none; }
    .gallery img.active { display: block; }
    .buttons { margin-bottom: 20px; }
  </style>
</head>
<body>
  <h1>Image Gallery with Filters</h1>
  <div class="buttons">
    <button onclick="filterImages('all')">All</button>
    <button onclick="filterImages('category1')">Category 1</button>
    <button onclick="filterImages('category2')">Category 2</button>
```

```
  </div>
  <div class="gallery">
    <img src="https://via.placeholder.com/200/ff7f7f/333333?text=Cat1-1" class="category1">
    <img src="https://via.placeholder.com/200/7fbfff/333333?text=Cat2-1" class="category2">
    <img src="https://via.placeholder.com/200/ff7f7f/333333?text=Cat1-2" class="category1">
    <img src="https://via.placeholder.com/200/7fbfff/333333?text=Cat2-2" class="category2">
  </div>
  <script>
    function filterImages(category) {
      const images = document.querySelectorAll('.gallery img');
      images.forEach(img => {
        img.classList.remove('active');
        if (category === 'all' || img.classList.contains(category)) {
          img.classList.add('active');
        }
      });
    }
    filterImages('all'); // Show all images by default
  </script>
</body>
</html>
```

Interactive Forms with Validation

```
<!DOCTYPE html>
<html lang="en">
<head>
  <meta charset="UTF-8">
  <meta name="viewport" content="width=device-width, initial-scale=1.0">
  <title>Interactive Forms with Validation</title>
  <style>
    body { font-family: Arial, sans-serif; }
```

```
    .error { color: red; display: none; }
  </style>
</head>
<body>
  <h1>Interactive Forms with Validation</h1>
  <form id="form" onsubmit="return validateForm()">
    <label for="name">Name:</label>
    <input type="text" id="name">
    <div id="nameError" class="error">Name is required</div>
    <br><br>
    <label for="email">Email:</label>
    <input type="text" id="email">
    <div id="emailError" class="error">Valid email is required</div>
    <br><br>
    <input type="submit" value="Submit">
  </form>
  <script>
    function validateForm() {
      let valid = true;
      const name = document.getElementById('name').value;
      const email = document.getElementById('email').value;
      const nameError = document.getElementById('nameError');
      const emailError = document.getElementById('emailError');
      nameError.style.display = 'none';
      emailError.style.display = 'none';
      if (name === '') {
        nameError.style.display = 'block';
        valid = false;
      }
```

```
      const emailPattern = /^[^ ]+@[^ ]+\.[a-z]{2,3}$/;
      if (!email.match(emailPattern)) {
        emailError.style.display = 'block';
        valid = false;
      }

      return valid;
    }
  </script>
</body>
</html>
```

Progress Bar

```
<!DOCTYPE html>
<html lang="en">
<head>
  <meta charset="UTF-8">
  <meta name="viewport" content="width=device-width, initial-scale=1.0">
  <title>Progress Bar</title>
  <style>
    body { font-family: Arial, sans-serif; text-align: center; }
    .progress-container { width: 80%; background: #ccc; border-radius: 25px; margin: 20px auto; padding: 3px; }
    .progress-bar { width: 0; height: 30px; background: #4caf50; border-radius: 25px; text-align: center; line-height: 30px; color: white; }
  </style>
</head>
<body>
  <h1>Progress Bar</h1>
  <div class="progress-container">
    <div class="progress-bar" id="progressBar">0%</div>
```

```
  </div>
  <button onclick="move()">Start</button>
  <script>
    function move() {
      const elem = document.getElementById("progressBar");
      let width = 0;
      const id = setInterval(frame, 20);
      function frame() {
        if (width >= 100) {
          clearInterval(id);
        } else {
          width++;
          elem.style.width = width + '%';
          elem.innerHTML = width + '%';
        }
      }
    }
  </script>
</body>
</html>
```

2.ANIMATIONS AND EFFECTS

Fading Text

```
<!DOCTYPE html>
<html lang="en">
<head>
  <meta charset="UTF-8">
  <meta name="viewport" content="width=device-width, initial-scale=1.0">
  <title>Fading Text</title>
  <style>
    body { font-family: Arial, sans-serif; text-align: center; }
    .fade-text { opacity: 0; transition: opacity 2s; }
    .fade-text.show { opacity: 1; }
  </style>
</head>
<body>
  <h1>Fading Text</h1>
  <div id="text" class="fade-text">This text will fade in and out.</div>
  <button onclick="toggleFade()">Toggle Fade</button>
  <script>
    function toggleFade() {
      const text = document.getElementById('text');
      text.classList.toggle('show');
    }
  </script>
</body>
</html>
```

Image Carousel with Animations

```
<!DOCTYPE html>
<html lang="en">
<head>
```

```
  <meta charset="UTF-8">
  <meta name="viewport" content="width=device-width, initial-scale=1.0">
  <title>Image Carousel with Animations</title>
  <style>
    body { font-family: Arial, sans-serif; text-align: center; }
    .carousel { position: relative; width: 80%; max-width: 800px; margin: auto; overflow: hidden;
}
    .carousel-images { display: flex; transition: transform 0.5s ease-in-out; }
    .carousel-images img { width: 100%; border-radius: 10px; }
    .navigation { position: absolute; top: 50%; width: 100%; display: flex; justify-content: space-
between; transform: translateY(-50%); }
    .prev, .next { background-color: rgba(0, 0, 0, 0.5); color: white; padding: 10px; border: none;
cursor: pointer; border-radius: 50%; }
  </style>
</head>
<body>
  <h1>Image Carousel with Animations</h1>
  <div class="carousel">
    <div class="carousel-images">
      <img src="https://via.placeholder.com/800x400/ff7f7f/333333?text=Image+1" alt="Image
1">
      <img src="https://via.placeholder.com/800x400/7fbfff/333333?text=Image+2" alt="Image
2">
      <img src="https://via.placeholder.com/800x400/7fff7f/333333?text=Image+3" alt="Image
3">
    </div>
    <div class="navigation">
      <button class="prev" onclick="prevSlide()">□ </button>
      <button class="next" onclick="nextSlide()">□ </button>
    </div>
```

```
  </div>
  <script>
    let currentIndex = 0;
    const images = document.querySelector('.carousel-images');
    const totalImages = document.querySelectorAll('.carousel-images img').length;
    function showSlide(index) {
      if (index >= totalImages) {
        currentIndex = 0;
      } else if (index < 0) {
        currentIndex = totalImages - 1;
      } else {
        currentIndex = index;
      }
      const offset = -currentIndex * 100;
      images.style.transform = `translateX(${offset}%)`;
    }

    function nextSlide() {
      showSlide(currentIndex + 1);
    }

    function prevSlide() {
      showSlide(currentIndex - 1);
    }

    setInterval(nextSlide, 3000); // Change image every 3 seconds
  </script>
</body>
</html>
```

Pop-up Notifications

```
<!DOCTYPE html>
<html lang="en">
<head>
  <meta charset="UTF-8">
  <meta name="viewport" content="width=device-width, initial-scale=1.0">
  <title>Pop-up Notifications</title>
  <style>
    body { font-family: Arial, sans-serif; text-align: center; }
    .notification { display: none; position: fixed; bottom: 20px; right: 20px; background: #4caf50;
color: white; padding: 15px; border-radius:
10px; box-shadow: 0 0 10px rgba(0, 0, 0, 0.1); }
.notification.show { display: block; }
</style>
</head>
<body>
  <h1>Pop-up Notifications</h1>
  <button onclick="showNotification()">Show Notification</button>
  <div id="notification" class="notification">This is a pop-up notification!</div>
  <script>
    function showNotification() {
      const notification = document.getElementById('notification');
      notification.classList.add('show');
      setTimeout(() => {
        notification.classList.remove('show');
      }, 3000); // Hide after 3 seconds
    }
  </script>
</body>
</html>
```

Text Scrolling

```
<!DOCTYPE html>
<html lang="en">
<head>
  <meta charset="UTF-8">
  <meta name="viewport" content="width=device-width, initial-scale=1.0">
  <title>Text Scrolling</title>
  <style>
    body { font-family: Arial, sans-serif; text-align: center; }
    .scrolling-text { overflow: hidden; white-space: nowrap; }
    .scrolling-text span { display: inline-block; padding-left: 100%; animation: scroll 10s linear
infinite; }
    @keyframes scroll {
      0% { transform: translateX(0); }
      100% { transform: translateX(-100%); }
    }
  </style>
</head>
<body>
  <h1>Text Scrolling</h1>
  <div class="scrolling-text">
    <span>This is a scrolling text example that moves continuously from right to left.</span>
  </div>
</body>
</html>
```

Particle Effects

```
<!DOCTYPE html>
<html lang="en">
<head>
  <meta charset="UTF-8">
```

```
  <meta name="viewport" content="width=device-width, initial-scale=1.0">
  <title>Particle Effects</title>
  <style>
    body { margin: 0; overflow: hidden; background: #000; }
    canvas { display: block; }
  </style>
</head>
<body>
  <h1>Particle Effects</h1>
  <canvas id="particlesCanvas"></canvas>
  <script>
    const canvas = document.getElementById('particlesCanvas');
    const ctx = canvas.getContext('2d');
    let particlesArray = [];
    canvas.width = window.innerWidth;
    canvas.height = window.innerHeight;
    class Particle {
      constructor() {
        this.x = Math.random() * canvas.width;
        this.y = Math.random() * canvas.height;
        this.size = Math.random() * 5 + 1;
        this.speedX = Math.random() * 3 - 1.5;
        this.speedY = Math.random() * 3 - 1.5;
      }
      update() {
        this.x += this.speedX;
        this.y += this.speedY;
        if (this.size > 0.2) this.size -= 0.1;
      }
      draw() {
```

```
        ctx.fillStyle = 'white';
        ctx.beginPath();
        ctx.arc(this.x, this.y, this.size, 0, Math.PI * 2);
        ctx.closePath();
        ctx.fill();
      }
    }
    function init() {
      particlesArray = [];
      for (let i = 0; i < 100; i++) {
        particlesArray.push(new Particle());
      }
    }
    function animate() {
      ctx.clearRect(0, 0, canvas.width, canvas.height);
      for (let i = 0; i < particlesArray.length; i++) {
        particlesArray[i].update();
        particlesArray[i].draw();
      }
      requestAnimationFrame(animate);
    }
    window.addEventListener('resize', () => {
      canvas.width = window.innerWidth;
      canvas.height = window.innerHeight;
      init();
    });
    init();
    animate();
  </script>
</body></html>
```

Menu with Hover Effects

```
<!DOCTYPE html>
<html lang="en">
<head>
  <meta charset="UTF-8">
  <meta name="viewport" content="width=device-width, initial-scale=1.0">
  <title>Menu with Hover Effects</title>
  <style>
    body { font-family: Arial, sans-serif; text-align: center; }
    .menu { display: flex; justify-content: center; list-style: none; padding: 0; }
    .menu li { margin: 0 15px; }
    .menu li a { text-decoration: none; color: black; padding: 10px 15px; transition: color 0.3s,
background 0.3s; }
    .menu li a:hover { color: white; background: black; border-radius: 5px; }
  </style>
</head>
<body>
  <h1>Menu with Hover Effects</h1>
  <ul class="menu">
    <li><a href="#">Home</a></li>
    <li><a href="#">About</a></li>
    <li><a href="#">Services</a></li>
    <li><a href="#">Contact</a></li>
  </ul>
</body>
</html>
```

Button Click Animations

```
<!DOCTYPE html>
<html lang="en">
<head>
```

```
  <meta charset="UTF-8">
  <meta name="viewport" content="width=device-width, initial-scale=1.0">
  <title>Button Click Animations</title>
  <style>
    body { font-family: Arial, sans-serif; text-align: center; margin-top: 50px; }
    .button { padding: 10px 20px; font-size: 16px; cursor: pointer; border: none; color: white; background: #007BFF; border-radius: 5px; transition: background 0.3s; position: relative; overflow: hidden; }
    .button:before { content: ''; position: absolute; top: 50%; left: 50%; width: 300%; height: 300%; background: rgba(255, 255, 255, 0.4); transform: translate(-50%, -50%) scale(0); border-radius: 50%; transition: transform 0.5s ease-out; }
    .button:active:before { transform: translate(-50%, -50%) scale(1); }
  </style>
</head>
<body>
  <h1>Button Click Animations</h1>
  <button class="button">Click Me</button>
</body>
</html>
```

Image Transitions (Slide, Fade)

```
<!DOCTYPE html>
<html lang="en">
<head>
  <meta charset="UTF-8">
  <meta name="viewport" content="width=device-width, initial-scale=1.0">
  <title>Image Transitions (Slide, Fade)</title>
  <style>
    body { font-family: Arial, sans-serif; text-align: center; }
    .slideshow-container { position: relative; max-width: 800px; margin: auto; }
    .fade { animation-name: fade; animation-duration: 1.5s; }
```

```
  @keyframes fade {
   from { opacity: .4; }
   to { opacity: 1; }
  }
  .mySlides { display: none; }
  .prev, .next { cursor: pointer; position: absolute; top: 50%; width: auto; margin-top: -22px;
padding: 16px; color: white; font-weight: bold; font-size: 20px; transition: 0.6s ease; border-
radius: 0 3px 3px 0; user-select: none; }
  .next { right: 0; border-radius: 3px 0 0 3px; }
  .prev:hover, .next:hover { background-color: rgba(0, 0, 0, 0.8); }
  .text { color: #f2f2f2; font-size: 15px; padding: 8px 12px; position: absolute; bottom: 8px;
width: 100%; text-align: center; }
 </style>
</head>
<body>
<h2>Image Slideshow with Fade Effect</h2>
<div class="slideshow-container">
 <div class="mySlides fade">
  <img src="https://via.placeholder.com/800x400/ff7f7f/333333?text=Slide+1"
style="width:100%">
  <div class="text">Caption Text 1</div>
 </div>
 <div class="mySlides fade">
  <img src="https://via.placeholder.com/800x400/7fbfff/333333?text=Slide+2"
style="width:100%">
  <div class="text">Caption Text 2</div>
 </div>
 <div class="mySlides fade">
  <img src="https://via.placeholder.com/800x400/7fff7f/333333?text=Slide+3"
style="width:100%">
```

```
    <div class="text">Caption Text 3</div>
  </div>
  <a class="prev" onclick="plusSlides(-1)">&#10094;</a>
  <a class="next" onclick="plusSlides(1)">&#10095;</a>
</div>
<br>
<script>
  let slideIndex = 0;
  showSlides();
  function showSlides() {
    let i;
    const slides = document.getElementsByClassName("mySlides");
    for (i = 0; i < slides.length; i++) {
      slides[i].style.display = "none";
    }
    slideIndex++;
    if (slideIndex > slides.length) {slideIndex = 1}
    slides[slideIndex-1].style.display = "block";
    setTimeout(showSlides, 2000); // Change image every 2 seconds
  }
  function plusSlides(n) {
    showSlides(slideIndex += n);
  }
</script>
</body>
</html>
```

Simple Game Animation

```
<!DOCTYPE html>
<html lang="en">
<head>
```

```
  <meta charset="UTF-8">
  <meta name="viewport" content="width=device-width, initial-scale=1.0">
  <title>Simple Game Animation</title>
  <style>
    body { font-family: Arial, sans-serif; text-align: center; }
    canvas { border: 1px solid black; }
  </style>
</head>
<body>
<h2>Simple Game Animation</h2>
<canvas id="myCanvas" width="480" height="320"></canvas>
<script>
  const canvas = document.getElementById("myCanvas");
  const ctx = canvas.getContext("2d");
  let x = canvas.width / 2;
  let y = canvas.height - 30;
  let dx = 2;
  let dy = -2;
  const ballRadius = 10;
  function drawBall() {
    ctx.beginPath();
    ctx.arc(x, y, ballRadius, 0, Math.PI * 2);
    ctx.fillStyle = "#0095DD";
    ctx.fill();
    ctx.closePath();
  }
  function draw() {
    ctx.clearRect(0, 0, canvas.width, canvas.height);
    drawBall();
    x += dx;
```

```
    y += dy;
    if (x + dx > canvas.width - ballRadius || x + dx < ballRadius) {
      dx = -dx;
    }
    if (y + dy > canvas.height - ballRadius || y + dy < ballRadius) {
      dy = -dy;
    }
  }
  setInterval(draw, 10);
</script>
</body>
</html>
```

3.DATA VISUALIZATION

Bar Chart

```
<!DOCTYPE html>
<html lang="en">
<head>
  <meta charset="UTF-8">
  <meta name="viewport" content="width=device-width, initial-scale=1.0">
  <title>Bar Chart</title>
  <script src="https://cdn.jsdelivr.net/npm/chart.js"></script>
</head>
<body>
  <h1>Bar Chart</h1>
  <canvas id="barChart"></canvas>
  <script>
    const ctx = document.getElementById('barChart').getContext('2d');
    const barChart = new Chart(ctx, {
      type: 'bar',
      data: {
        labels: ['January', 'February', 'March', 'April', 'May', 'June'],
        datasets: [{
          label: 'Sales',
          backgroundColor: 'rgba(54, 162, 235, 0.2)',
          borderColor: 'rgba(54, 162, 235, 1)',
          borderWidth: 1,
          data: [65, 59, 80, 81, 56, 55]
        }]
      },
      options: {
        scales: {
          y: {
```

```
          beginAtZero: true
        }
      }
    }
  });
</script>
</body>
</html>
```

Pie Chart

```
<!DOCTYPE html>
<html lang="en">
<head>
  <meta charset="UTF-8">
  <meta name="viewport" content="width=device-width, initial-scale=1.0">
  <title>Pie Chart</title>
  <script src="https://cdn.jsdelivr.net/npm/chart.js"></script>
</head>
<body>
  <h1>Pie Chart</h1>
  <canvas id="pieChart"></canvas>
  <script>
    const ctx = document.getElementById('pieChart').getContext('2d');
    const pieChart = new Chart(ctx, {
      type: 'pie',
      data: {
        labels: ['Red', 'Blue', 'Yellow', 'Green', 'Purple', 'Orange'],
        datasets: [{
          label: 'My First Dataset',
          data: [12, 19, 3, 5, 2, 3],
          backgroundColor: [
```

```
          'rgba(255, 99, 132, 0.2)',
          'rgba(54, 162, 235, 0.2)',
          'rgba(255, 206, 86, 0.2)',
          'rgba(75, 192, 192, 0.2)',
          'rgba(153, 102, 255, 0.2)',
          'rgba(255, 159, 64, 0.2)'
        ],
        borderColor: [
          'rgba(255, 99, 132, 1)',
          'rgba(54, 162, 235, 1)',
          'rgba(255, 206, 86, 1)',
          'rgba(75, 192, 192, 1)',
          'rgba(153, 102, 255, 1)',
          'rgba(255, 159, 64, 1)'
        ],
        borderWidth: 1
      }]
    }
  });
  </script>
</body>
</html>
```

Line Chart

```
<!DOCTYPE html>
<html lang="en">
<head>
  <meta charset="UTF-8">
  <meta name="viewport" content="width=device-width, initial-scale=1.0">
  <title>Line Chart</title>
  <script src="https://cdn.jsdelivr.net/npm/chart.js"></script>
```

```
</head>
<body>
  <h1>Line Chart</h1>
  <canvas id="lineChart"></canvas>
  <script>
    const ctx = document.getElementById('lineChart').getContext('2d');
    const lineChart = new Chart(ctx, {
      type: 'line',
      data: {
        labels: ['January', 'February', 'March', 'April', 'May', 'June'],
        datasets: [{
          label: 'Sales',
          data: [65, 59, 80, 81, 56, 55],
          borderColor: 'rgba(54, 162, 235, 1)',
          borderWidth: 1,
          fill: false
        }]
      },
      options: {
        scales: {
          y: {
            beginAtZero: true
          }
        }
      }
    });
  </script>
</body>
</html>
```

Real-time Data Update

```
<!DOCTYPE html>
<html lang="en">
<head>
  <meta charset="UTF-8">
  <meta name="viewport" content="width=device-width, initial-scale=1.0">
  <title>Real-time Data Update</title>
  <script src="https://cdn.jsdelivr.net/npm/chart.js"></script>
</head>
<body>
  <h1>Real-time Data Update</h1>
  <canvas id="realTimeChart"></canvas>
  <script>
    const ctx = document.getElementById('realTimeChart').getContext('2d');
    const realTimeChart = new Chart(ctx, {
      type: 'line',
      data: {
        labels: [],
        datasets: [{
          label: 'Real-time Data',
          data: [],
          borderColor: 'rgba(54, 162, 235, 1)',
          borderWidth: 1,
          fill: false
        }]
      },
      options: {
        animation: false,
        scales: {
          y: {
```

```
          beginAtZero: true
        }
      }
    }
  });
  setInterval(() => {
    const now = new Date();
    realTimeChart.data.labels.push(now.toLocaleTimeString());
    realTimeChart.data.datasets[0].data.push(Math.random() * 100);
    realTimeChart.update();
  }, 1000);
 </script>
</body>
</html>
```

Interactive Map

```
<!DOCTYPE html>
<html lang="en">
<head>
 <meta charset="UTF-8">
 <meta name="viewport" content="width=device-width, initial-scale=1.0">
 <title>Interactive Map</title>
 <style>
   #map { height: 400px; width: 100%; }
 </style>
 <script
src="https://maps.googleapis.com/maps/api/js?key=YOUR_API_KEY&callback=initMap"
async defer></script>
 <script>
   function initMap() {
     const myLatLng = { lat: -25.363, lng: 131.044 };
```

```
    const map = new google.maps.Map(document.getElementById("map"), {
     zoom: 4,
     center: myLatLng,
    });
    new google.maps.Marker({
     position: myLatLng,
     map,
     title: "Hello World!",
    });
   }
  </script>
</head>
<body>
  <h1>Interactive Map</h1>
  <div id="map"></div>
</body>
</html>
```

4.GAMES AND APPLICATIONS

Memory Game

```
<!DOCTYPE html>
<html lang="en">
<head>
  <meta charset="UTF-8">
  <meta name="viewport" content="width=device-width, initial-scale=1.0">
  <title>Memory Game</title>
  <style>
    body { font-family: Arial, sans-serif; }
    .grid { display: flex; flex-wrap: wrap; width: 200px; }
    .card { width: 50px; height: 50px; background: lightgray; margin: 5px; display: flex; justify-content: center; align-items: center; font-size: 24px; }
    .hidden { background: darkgray; color: darkgray; }
  </style>
</head>
<body>
  <h1>Memory Game</h1>
  <div class="grid" id="grid"></div>
  <script>
    const cardsArray = ['A', 'B', 'C', 'D', 'A', 'B', 'C', 'D'];
    let shuffledCards = cardsArray.sort(() => 0.5 - Math.random());
    const grid = document.getElementById('grid');
    let firstCard = null;
    let secondCard = null;
    shuffledCards.forEach((card) => {
      const cardElement = document.createElement('div');
      cardElement.classList.add('card', 'hidden');
      cardElement.textContent = card;
      cardElement.addEventListener('click', flipCard);
```

```
      grid.appendChild(cardElement);
    });

    function flipCard() {
      if (this.classList.contains('hidden')) {
        this.classList.remove('hidden');
        if (!firstCard) {
          firstCard = this;
        } else if (!secondCard) {
          secondCard = this;
          checkMatch();
        }
      }
    }

    function checkMatch() {
      if (firstCard.textContent === secondCard.textContent) {
        firstCard = null;
        secondCard = null;
      } else {
        setTimeout(() => {
          firstCard.classList.add('hidden');
          secondCard.classList.add('hidden');
          firstCard = null;
          secondCard = null;
        }, 1000);
      }
    }
  </script>
</body>
```

</html>

Tic-Tac-Toe

```
<!DOCTYPE html>
<html lang="en">
<head>
  <meta charset="UTF-8">
  <meta name="viewport" content="width=device-width, initial-scale=1.0">
  <title>Tic-Tac-Toe</title>
  <style>
    body { font-family: Arial, sans-serif; }
    .board { display: grid; grid-template-columns: repeat(3, 100px); grid-gap: 5px; }
    .cell { width: 100px; height: 100px; background: lightgray; display: flex; justify-content:
center; align-items: center; font-size: 36px; cursor: pointer; }
  </style>
</head>
<body>
  <h1>Tic-Tac-Toe</h1>
  <div class="board" id="board"></div>
  <script>
    const board = document.getElementById('board');
    let cells = Array(9).fill(null);
    let currentPlayer = 'X';
    cells.forEach((cell, index) => {
      const cellElement = document.createElement('div');
      cellElement.classList.add('cell');
      cellElement.addEventListener('click', () => makeMove(index));
      board.appendChild(cellElement);
    });
    function makeMove(index) {
      if (!cells[index]) {
```

```
        cells[index] = currentPlayer;
        updateBoard();
        currentPlayer = currentPlayer === 'X' ? 'O' : 'X';
        checkWin();
      }
    }
    function updateBoard() {
      board.childNodes.forEach((cell, index) => {
        cell.textContent = cells[index];
      });
    }
    function checkWin() {
      const winPatterns = [
        [0, 1, 2], [3, 4, 5], [6, 7, 8],
        [0, 3, 6], [1, 4, 7], [2, 5, 8],
        [0, 4, 8], [2, 4, 6]
      ];
      winPatterns.forEach(pattern => {
        const [a, b, c] = pattern;
        if (cells[a] && cells[a] === cells[b] && cells[a] === cells[c]) {
          setTimeout(() => alert(`Player ${cells[a]} wins!`), 10);
        }
      });
    }
  </script>
</body>
</html>
```

Simple Quiz

```
<!DOCTYPE html>
<html lang="en">
```

```
<head>
  <meta charset="UTF-8">
  <meta name="viewport" content="width=device-width, initial-scale=1.0">
  <title>Simple Quiz</title>
  <style>
    body { font-family: Arial, sans-serif; }
    .question { margin-bottom: 10px; }
    .answer { margin-bottom: 5px; }
  </style>
</head>
<body>
  <h1>Simple Quiz</h1>
  <div id="quiz"></div>
  <button onclick="submitQuiz()">Submit</button>
  <p id="result"></p>
  <script>
    const questions = [
      { question: "What is 2 + 2?", answers: ["3", "4", "5"], correct: 1 },
      { question: "What is the capital of France?", answers: ["Berlin", "Madrid", "Paris"], correct:
2 },
    ];

    const quiz = document.getElementById('quiz');

    questions.forEach((q, index) => {
      const questionElement = document.createElement('div');
      questionElement.classList.add('question');
      questionElement.innerHTML = `<p>${q.question}</p>`;
      q.answers.forEach((answer, i) => {
        const answerElement = document.createElement('div');
```

```
        answerElement.classList.add('answer');
        answerElement.innerHTML = `<input type="radio" name="q${index}" value="${i}">
${answer}`;
        questionElement.appendChild(answerElement);
      });
      quiz.appendChild(questionElement);
    });

    function submitQuiz() {
      let score = 0;
      questions.forEach((q, index) => {
        const selected = document.querySelector(`input[name="q${index}"]:checked`);
        if (selected && parseInt(selected.value) === q.correct) {
          score++;
        }
      });
      document.getElementById('result').textContent = `Your score:
${score}/${questions.length}`;
    }
  </script>
</body>
</html>
```

Hangman

```
<!DOCTYPE html>
<html lang="en">
<head>
  <meta charset="UTF-8">
  <meta name="viewport" content="width=device-width, initial-scale=1.0">
  <title>Hangman</title>
  <style>
```

```
    body { font-family: Arial, sans-serif; }
    .letter { font-size: 24px; margin-right: 5px; }
  </style>
</head>
<body>
  <h1>Hangman</h1>
  <p id="word"></p>
  <input type="text" id="guess" maxlength="1">
  <button onclick="makeGuess()">Guess</button>
  <p id="message"></p>
  <script>
    const word = "JAVASCRIPT";
    let guessedWord = Array(word.length).fill('_');
    let attempts = 0;

    document.getElementById('word').textContent = guessedWord.join(' ');

    function makeGuess() {
      const guess = document.getElementById('guess').value.toUpperCase();
      if (guess) {
        let found = false;
        for (let i = 0; i < word.length; i++) {
          if (word[i] === guess) {
            guessedWord[i] = guess;
            found = true;
          }
        }
        document.getElementById('word').textContent = guessedWord.join(' ');
        document.getElementById('guess').value = '';
        if (!found) attempts++;
```

```
        if (guessedWord.join('') === word) {
          document.getElementById('message').textContent = 'You win!';
        } else if (attempts >= 6) {
          document.getElementById('message').textContent = 'You lose!';
        }
      }
    }
  </script>
</body>
</html>
```

Color Guessing Game

```
<!DOCTYPE html>
<html lang="en">
<head>
  <meta charset="UTF-8">
  <meta name="viewport" content="width
="width=device-width, initial-scale=1.0">

  <title>Color Guessing Game</title>
  <style>
    body { font-family: Arial, sans-serif; text-align: center; }
    .color-box { width: 100px; height: 100px; display: inline-block; margin: 10px; cursor: pointer;
}
  </style>
</head>
<body>
  <h1>Color Guessing Game</h1>
  <p id="colorDisplay"></p>
  <div id="colorGrid"></div>
  <p id="message"></p>
```

```
  <script>
    const colors = ['red', 'green', 'blue', 'yellow', 'purple', 'orange'];
    const correctColor = colors[Math.floor(Math.random() * colors.length)];
    document.getElementById('colorDisplay').textContent = `Guess the color: ${correctColor}`;
colors.forEach(color => {
  const colorBox = document.createElement('div');
  colorBox.classList.add('color-box');
  colorBox.style.backgroundColor = color;
  colorBox.addEventListener('click', () => checkColor(color));
  document.getElementById('colorGrid').appendChild(colorBox);
});
function checkColor(color) {
  if (color === correctColor) {
    document.getElementById('message').textContent = 'Correct!';
  } else {
    document.getElementById('message').textContent = 'Try Again!';
  }
}
  </script>
</body>
</html>
```

To-Do List Application

```
<!DOCTYPE html>
<html lang="en">
<head>
  <meta charset="UTF-8">
  <meta name="viewport" content="width=device-width, initial-scale=1.0">
  <title>To-Do List Application</title>
  <style>
    body { font-family: Arial, sans-serif; }
```

```
    ul { list-style-type: none; padding: 0; }
    li { padding: 8px; margin: 5px 0; background: #f4f4f4; display: flex; justify-content: space-between; }
  </style>
</head>
<body>
  <h1>To-Do List</h1>
  <input type="text" id="taskInput" placeholder="New task">
  <button onclick="addTask()">Add</button>
  <ul id="taskList"></ul>
  <script>
    function addTask() {
      const taskInput = document.getElementById('taskInput');
      const task = taskInput.value;
      if (task) {
        const li = document.createElement('li');
        li.textContent = task;
        const removeButton = document.createElement('button');
        removeButton.textContent = 'Remove';
        removeButton.onclick = () => li.remove();
        li.appendChild(removeButton);
        document.getElementById('taskList').appendChild(li);
        taskInput.value = '';
      }
    }
  </script>
</body>
</html>
```

Countdown Timer

```
<!DOCTYPE html>
<html lang="en">
<head>
  <meta charset="UTF-8">
  <meta name="viewport" content="width=device-width, initial-scale=1.0">
  <title>Countdown Timer</title>
  <style>
    body { font-family: Arial, sans-serif; text-align: center; }
    #time { font-size: 48px; }
  </style>
</head>
<body>
  <h1>Countdown Timer</h1>
  <input type="number" id="minutes" placeholder="Minutes">
  <button onclick="startTimer()">Start</button>
  <div id="time">00:00</div>
  <script>
    let countdown;
    function startTimer() {
      clearInterval(countdown);
      const minutes = document.getElementById('minutes').value;
      const now = Date.now();
      const then = now + minutes * 60000;
      displayTimeLeft(minutes * 60);

      countdown = setInterval(() => {
        const secondsLeft = Math.round((then - Date.now()) / 1000);
        if (secondsLeft <= 0) {
          clearInterval(countdown);
```

```
        document.getElementById('time').textContent = '00:00';
        alert('Time is up!');
        return;
      }
      displayTimeLeft(secondsLeft);
    }, 1000);
  }

  function displayTimeLeft(seconds) {
    const minutes = Math.floor(seconds / 60);
    const remainderSeconds = seconds % 60;
    const display = `${minutes < 10 ? '0' : ''}${minutes}:${remainderSeconds < 10 ? '0' :
''}${remainderSeconds}`;
    document.getElementById('time').textContent = display;
  }
 </script>
</body>
</html>
```

Simple Drawing Application

```
<!DOCTYPE html>
<html lang="en">
<head>
 <meta charset="UTF-8">
 <meta name="viewport" content="width=device-width, initial-scale=1.0">
 <title>Simple Drawing Application</title>
 <style>
   body { font-family: Arial, sans-serif; }
   #canvas { border: 1px solid black; }
 </style>
</head>
```

```
<body>
  <h1>Simple Drawing Application</h1>
  <canvas id="canvas" width="500" height="500"></canvas>
  <script>
    const canvas = document.getElementById('canvas');
    const context = canvas.getContext('2d');
    let drawing = false;

    canvas.addEventListener('mousedown', () => { drawing = true; });
    canvas.addEventListener('mouseup', () => { drawing = false; context.beginPath(); });
    canvas.addEventListener('mousemove', draw);

    function draw(event) {
      if (!drawing) return;
      context.lineWidth = 5;
      context.lineCap = 'round';
      context.strokeStyle = 'black';
      context.lineTo(event.clientX - canvas.offsetLeft, event.clientY - canvas.offsetTop);
      context.stroke();
      context.beginPath();
      context.moveTo(event.clientX - canvas.offsetLeft, event.clientY - canvas.offsetTop);
    }
  </script>
</body>
</html>
```

Weather App (Data fetched from external source)

```
<!DOCTYPE html>
<html lang="en">
<head>
  <meta charset="UTF-8">
```

```
  <meta name="viewport" content="width=device-width, initial-scale=1.0">
  <title>Weather App</title>
  <style>
    body { font-family: Arial, sans-serif; text-align: center; }
    #weather { margin-top: 50px; }
  </style>
</head>
<body>
  <h1>Weather App</h1>
  <div id="weather"></div>
  <script>
  fetch('https://api.openweathermap.org/data/2.5/weather?q=London&appid=YOUR_API_KEY')
      .then(response => response.json())
      .then(data => {
        const weatherDiv = document.getElementById('weather');
        weatherDiv.innerHTML = `
          <h2>${data.name}, ${data.sys.country}</h2>
          <p>Temperature: ${(data.main.temp - 273.15).toFixed(2)} °C</p>
          <p>Description: ${data.weather[0].description}</p>
        `;
      })
      .catch(error => {
        console.error('Error fetching weather data:', error);
      });
  </script>
</body>
</html>
```

Currency Converter

```
<!DOCTYPE html>
<html lang="en">
```

```
<head>
  <meta charset="UTF-8">
  <meta name="viewport" content="width=device-width, initial-scale=1.0">
  <title>Currency Converter</title>
  <style>
    body { font-family: Arial, sans-serif; text-align: center; }
    #converter { margin-top: 50px; }
  </style>
</head>
<body>
  <h1>Currency Converter</h1>
  <div id="converter">
    <input type="number" id="amount" placeholder="Enter amount">
    <select id="from">
      <option value="USD">USD</option>
      <option value="EUR">EUR</option>
      <option value="GBP">GBP</option>
    </select>
    <select id="to">
      <option value="USD">USD</option>
      <option value="EUR">EUR</option>
      <option value="GBP">GBP</option>
    </select>
    <button onclick="convert()">Convert</button>
    <p id="result"></p>
  </div>
  <script>
    function convert() {
      const amount = document.getElementById('amount').value;
      const from = document.getElementById('from').value;
```

```
      const to = document.getElementById('to').value;
      fetch(`https://api.exchangerate-api.com/v4/latest/${from}`)
        .then(response => response.json())
        .then(data => {
          const rate = data.rates[to];
          const result = (amount * rate).toFixed(2);
          document.getElementById('result').textContent = `${amount} ${from} = ${result} ${to}`;
        })
        .catch(error => {
          console.error('Error fetching exchange rates:', error);
        });
    }
  </script>
</body></html>
```

5.USER INTERACTION

Image Cropper

```
<!DOCTYPE html>
<html lang="en">
<head>
  <meta charset="UTF-8">
  <meta name="viewport" content="width=device-width, initial-scale=1.0">
  <title>Image Cropper</title>
  <style>
    #container { width: 500px; margin: 50px auto; }
    #image { max-width: 100%; }
  </style>
</head>
<body>
  <h1>Image Cropper</h1>
  <div id="container">
    <input type="file" accept="image/*" id="fileInput">
    <br>
    <canvas id="canvas" width="400" height="300"></canvas>
    <br>
    <button onclick="crop()">Crop Image</button>
  </div>

  <script>
    const fileInput = document.getElementById('fileInput');
    const canvas = document.getElementById('canvas');
    const ctx = canvas.getContext('2d');

    fileInput.addEventListener('change', (e) => {
      const file = e.target.files[0];
```

```
      const reader = new FileReader();

      reader.onload = (event) => {
        const img = new Image();
        img.onload = () => {
          canvas.width = img.width;
          canvas.height = img.height;
          ctx.drawImage(img, 0, 0);
        };
        img.src = event.target.result;
      };
      reader.readAsDataURL(file);
    });

    function crop() {
      // Perform cropping operation
      // Example: ctx.drawImage(img, sx, sy, sw, sh, dx, dy, dw, dh);
    }
  </script>
</body>
</html>
```

File Uploader

```
<!DOCTYPE html>
<html lang="en">
<head>
  <meta charset="UTF-8">
  <meta name="viewport" content="width=device-width, initial-scale=1.0">
  <title>File Uploader</title>
</head>
<body>
```

```
  <h1>File Uploader</h1>
  <input type="file" id="fileInput">
  <button onclick="upload()">Upload</button>

  <script>
    function upload() {
      const fileInput = document.getElementById('fileInput');
      const file = fileInput.files[0];
      if (file) {
        // Perform file upload operation
        console.log('Uploading file:', file);
      } else {
        console.error('No file selected.');
      }
    }
  </script>
</body>
</html>
```

Chat Application (basic)

```
<!DOCTYPE html>
<html lang="en">
<head>
  <meta charset="UTF-8">
  <meta name="viewport" content="width=device-width, initial-scale=1.0">
  <title>Chat Application</title>
</head>
<body>
  <h1>Chat Application</h1>
  <div id="chatBox" style="border: 1px solid black; height: 300px; overflow-y: scroll;"></div>
  <br>
```

```
  <input type="text" id="messageInput">
  <button onclick="sendMessage()">Send</button>
  <script>
    function sendMessage() {
      const messageInput = document.getElementById('messageInput');
      const message = messageInput.value.trim();
      if (message) {
        const chatBox = document.getElementById('chatBox');
        const newMessage = document.createElement('div');
        newMessage.textContent = message;
        chatBox.appendChild(newMessage);
        messageInput.value = '';
      }
    }
  </script>
</body>
</html>
```

Social Media Feed with Likes/Comments (basic)

```
<!DOCTYPE html>
<html lang="en">
<head>
  <meta charset="UTF-8">
  <meta name="viewport" content="width=device-width, initial-scale=1.0">
  <title>Social Media Feed</title>
  <style>
    .post { border: 1px solid #ccc; margin-bottom: 10px; padding: 10px; }
    .likes { color: blue; cursor: pointer; }
  </style>
</head>
<body>
```

```
<h1>Social Media Feed</h1>
<div class="post">
  <p>This is a post.</p>
  <button class="likes" onclick="likePost(this)">Like</button>
  <span class="likesCount">0</span>
  <br>
  <textarea placeholder="Write a comment"></textarea>
  <button onclick="postComment(this)">Comment</button>
  <div class="comments"></div>
</div>

<script>
  function likePost(button) {
    const likesCount = button.parentElement.querySelector('.likesCount');
    let count = parseInt(likesCount.textContent);
    count++;
    likesCount.textContent = count;
  }

  function postComment(button) {
    const textarea = button.parentElement.querySelector('textarea');
    const commentText = textarea.value.trim();
    if (commentText) {
      const commentsDiv = button.parentElement.querySelector('.comments');
      const newComment = document.createElement('div');
      newComment.textContent = commentText;
      commentsDiv.appendChild(newComment);
      textarea.value = '';
    }
  }
```

```
  </script>
</body>
</html>
```

Photo Editor (basic)

```
<!DOCTYPE html>
<html lang="en">
<head>
  <meta charset="UTF-8">
  <meta name="viewport" content="width=device-width, initial-scale=1.0">
  <title>Photo Editor</title>
  <style>
    #container { width: 500px; margin: 50px auto; text-align: center; }
    #canvas { border: 1px solid black; }
    button { margin: 10px; }
  </style>
</head>
<body>
  <h1>Photo Editor</h1>
  <div id="container">
    <input type="file" accept="image/*" id="fileInput">
    <br>
    <canvas id="canvas" width="400" height="300"></canvas>
    <br>
    <button onclick="applyFilter('grayscale')">Grayscale</button>
    <button onclick="applyFilter('sepia')">Sepia</button>
    <button onclick="applyFilter('invert')">Invert</button>
    <button onclick="resetImage()">Reset</button>
  </div>

  <script>
```

```
const fileInput = document.getElementById('fileInput');
const canvas = document.getElementById('canvas');
const ctx = canvas.getContext('2d');
let originalImage = null;

fileInput.addEventListener('change', (e) => {
 const file = e.target.files[0];
 const reader = new FileReader();

 reader.onload = (event) => {
  const img = new Image();
  img.onload = () => {
   canvas.width = img.width;
   canvas.height = img.height;
   ctx.drawImage(img, 0, 0);
   originalImage = ctx.getImageData(0, 0, canvas.width, canvas.height);
  };
  img.src = event.target.result;
 };
 reader.readAsDataURL(file);
});

function applyFilter(filter) {
 if (!originalImage) return;

 const imageData = ctx.getImageData(0, 0, canvas.width, canvas.height);
 const data = imageData.data;

 for (let i = 0; i < data.length; i += 4) {
  const r = data[i];
```

```
        const g = data[i + 1];
        const b = data[i + 2];

        if (filter === 'grayscale') {
          const avg = (r + g + b) / 3;
          data[i] = data[i + 1] = data[i + 2] = avg;
        } else if (filter === 'sepia') {
          data[i] = r * 0.393 + g * 0.769 + b * 0.189;
          data[i + 1] = r * 0.349 + g * 0.686 + b * 0.168;
          data[i + 2] = r * 0.272 + g * 0.534 + b * 0.131;
        } else if (filter === 'invert') {
          data[i] = 255 - r;
          data[i + 1] = 255 - g;
          data[i + 2] = 255 - b;
        }
      }

      ctx.putImageData(imageData, 0, 0);
    }

    function resetImage() {
      if (originalImage) {
        ctx.putImageData(originalImage, 0, 0);
      }
    }
  </script>
</body>
</html>
```

6.LEARNING AND REFERENCE

Color Picker

```
<!DOCTYPE html>
<html lang="en">
<head>
  <meta charset="UTF-8">
  <meta name="viewport" content="width=device-width, initial-scale=1.0">
  <title>Color Picker</title>
  <style>
    body { font-family: Arial, sans-serif; text-align: center; }
    #colorBox { width: 100px; height: 100px; margin: 20px auto; border: 1px solid black; }
  </style>
</head>
<body>
  <h1>Color Picker</h1>
  <input type="color" id="colorInput">
  <div id="colorBox"></div>
  <script>
    document.getElementById('colorInput').addEventListener('input', (e) => {
      const color = e.target.value;
      document.getElementById('colorBox').style.backgroundColor = color;
    });
  </script>
</body>
</html>
```

Unit Converter

```
<!DOCTYPE html>
<html lang="en">
<head>
  <meta charset="UTF-8">
```

```
  <meta name="viewport" content="width=device-width, initial-scale=1.0">
  <title>Unit Converter</title>
  <style>
    body { font-family: Arial, sans-serif; text-align: center; }
    .converter { margin: 20px; }
  </style>
</head>
<body>
  <h1>Unit Converter</h1>
  <div class="converter">
    <input type="number" id="inputValue" placeholder="Enter value">
    <select id="fromUnit">
      <option value="meters">Meters</option>
      <option value="kilometers">Kilometers</option>
      <option value="feet">Feet</option>
      <option value="miles">Miles</option>
    </select>
    <select id="toUnit">
      <option value="meters">Meters</option>
      <option value="kilometers">Kilometers</option>
      <option value="feet">Feet</option>
      <option value="miles">Miles</option>
    </select>
    <button onclick="convert()">Convert</button>
    <p id="result"></p>
  </div>
  <script>
    function convert() {
      const inputValue = parseFloat(document.getElementById('inputValue').value);
      const fromUnit = document.getElementById('fromUnit').value;
```

```
      const toUnit = document.getElementById('toUnit').value;
      const conversionRates = {
        meters: { meters: 1, kilometers: 0.001, feet: 3.28084, miles: 0.000621371 },
        kilometers: { meters: 1000, kilometers: 1, feet: 3280.84, miles: 0.621371 },
        feet: { meters: 0.3048, kilometers: 0.0003048, feet: 1, miles: 0.000189394 },
        miles: { meters: 1609.34, kilometers: 1.60934, feet: 5280, miles: 1 }
      };
      const result = inputValue * conversionRates[fromUnit][toUnit];
      document.getElementById('result').textContent = `${inputValue} ${fromUnit} = ${result}
${toUnit}`;
    }
  </script>
</body>
</html>
```

Periodic Table with Element Information

```
<!DOCTYPE html>
<html lang="en">
<head>
  <meta charset="UTF-8">
  <meta name="viewport" content="width=device-width, initial-scale=1.0">
  <title>Periodic Table</title>
  <style>
    body { font-family: Arial, sans-serif; text-align: center; }
    .element { display: inline-block; border: 1px solid black; width: 50px; height: 50px; margin:
5px; padding: 5px; cursor: pointer; }
  </style>
</head>
<body>
  <h1>Periodic Table</h1>
  <div id="periodicTable">
```

```
    <div class="element" data-element="H" onclick="showInfo(this)">H</div>
    <div class="element" data-element="He" onclick="showInfo(this)">He</div>
    <!-- Add more elements as needed -->
  </div>
  <div id="elementInfo"></div>
  <script>
    const elementsInfo = {
      H: { name: 'Hydrogen', atomicNumber: 1, symbol: 'H' },
      He: { name: 'Helium', atomicNumber: 2, symbol: 'He' }
      // Add more elements as needed
    };
    function showInfo(element) {
      const elementSymbol = element.getAttribute('data-element');
      const info = elementsInfo[elementSymbol];
      document.getElementById('elementInfo').innerHTML = `
        <h2>${info.name} (${info.symbol})</h2>
        <p>Atomic Number: ${info.atomicNumber}</p>
      `;
    }
  </script>
</body>
</html>
```

Flashcards with Animations

```
<!DOCTYPE html>
<html lang="en">
<head>
  <meta charset="UTF-8">
  <meta name="viewport" content="width=device-width, initial-scale=1.0">
  <title>Flashcards</title>
  <style>
```

```
    body { font-family: Arial, sans-serif; text-align: center; }
    .flashcard { display: inline-block; border: 1px solid black; width: 200px; height: 150px;
margin: 20px; padding: 20px; cursor: pointer; transition: transform 0.5s; }
    .flashcard:hover { transform: rotateY(180deg); }
  </style>
</head>
<body>
  <h1>Flashcards</h1>
  <div class="flashcard" onclick="flipCard(this)">
    <div class="front">Question 1</div>
    <div class="back" style="display: none;">Answer 1</div>
  </div>
  <div class="flashcard" onclick="flipCard(this)">
    <div class="front">Question 2</div>
    <div class="back" style="display: none;">Answer 2</div>
  </div>
  <script>
    function flipCard(card) {
      const front = card.querySelector('.front');
      const back = card.querySelector('.back');
      if (front.style.display !== 'none') {
        front.style.display = 'none';
        back.style.display = 'block';
      } else {
        front.style.display = 'block';
        back.style.display = 'none';
      }
    }
  </script>
</body> </html>
```

7.E-COMMERCE ELEMENTS

Product Slider with Details

```
<!DOCTYPE html>
<html lang="en">
<head>
  <meta charset="UTF-8">
  <meta name="viewport" content="width=device-width, initial-scale=1.0">
  <title>Product Slider with Details</title>
  <style>
    body { font-family: Arial, sans-serif; text-align: center; }
    .slider { display: flex; overflow: hidden; width: 300px; margin: 20px auto; }
    .slider img { width: 300px; height: 200px; }
    .details { margin-top: 20px; }
  </style>
</head>
<body>
  <h1>Product Slider</h1>
  <div class="slider" id="slider">
    <img src="product1.jpg" alt="Product 1">
    <img src="product2.jpg" alt="Product 2" style="display: none;">
    <img src="product3.jpg" alt="Product 3" style="display: none;">
  </div>
  <button onclick="prev()">Previous</button>
  <button onclick="next()">Next</button>
  <div class="details" id="details">
    <h2>Product 1</h2>
    <p>Details of Product 1</p>
  </div>
  <script>
    let currentIndex = 0;
```

```
    const images = document.querySelectorAll('.slider img');
    const details = [
      { title: 'Product 1', description: 'Details of Product 1' },
      { title: 'Product 2', description: 'Details of Product 2' },
      { title: 'Product 3', description: 'Details of Product 3' }
    ];
    function showSlide(index) {
      images.forEach((img, i) => img.style.display = i === index ? 'block' : 'none');
      document.getElementById('details').innerHTML = `
        <h2>${details[index].title}</h2>
        <p>${details[index].description}</p>
      `;
    }

    function prev() {
      currentIndex = (currentIndex - 1 + images.length) === images.length ? 0 : (currentIndex - 1
+ images.length) % images.length;
      showSlide(currentIndex);
    }

    function next() {
      currentIndex = (currentIndex + 1) % images.length;
      showSlide(currentIndex);
    }
  </script>
</body>
</html>
```

Shopping Cart with Update Functionality

```
<!DOCTYPE html>
<html lang="en">
```

```
<head>
  <meta charset="UTF-8">
  <meta name="viewport" content="width=device-width, initial-scale=1.0">
  <title>Shopping Cart</title>
  <style>
    body { font-family: Arial, sans-serif; }
    table { width: 80%; margin: 20px auto; border-collapse: collapse; }
    th, td { border: 1px solid #ddd; padding: 8px; text-align: center; }
    th { background-color: #f2f2f2; }
    .total { text-align: right; padding-right: 20px; }
  </style>
</head>
<body>
  <h1>Shopping Cart</h1>
  <table>
    <thead>
      <tr>
        <th>Product</th>
        <th>Price</th>
        <th>Quantity</th>
        <th>Total</th>
        <th>Actions</th>
      </tr>
    </thead>
    <tbody id="cartItems">
      <!-- Items will be dynamically added here -->
    </tbody>
  </table>
  <div class="total">
    <strong>Total: $<span id="totalPrice">0.00</span></strong>
```

```
  </div>
  <button onclick="checkout()">Checkout</button>

  <script>
    const cart = [
      { name: 'Product 1', price: 10.00, quantity: 1 },
      { name: 'Product 2', price: 20.00, quantity: 2 }
    ];

    function updateCart() {
      const cartItems = document.getElementById('cartItems');
      cartItems.innerHTML = '';
      let totalPrice = 0;

      cart.forEach((item, index) => {
        const itemTotal = item.price * item.quantity;
        totalPrice += itemTotal;

        const row = document.createElement('tr');
        row.innerHTML = `
          <td>${item.name}</td>
          <td>$${item.price.toFixed(2)}</td>
          <td><input type="number" value="${item.quantity}" min="1"
onchange="updateQuantity(${index}, this.value)"></td>
          <td>$${itemTotal.toFixed(2)}</td>
          <td><button onclick="removeItem(${index})">Remove</button></td>
        `;
        cartItems.appendChild(row);
      });
```

```
      document.getElementById('totalPrice').textContent = totalPrice.toFixed(2);
    }
    function updateQuantity(index, quantity) {
      cart[index].quantity = parseInt(quantity);
      updateCart();
    }
    function removeItem(index) {
      cart.splice(index, 1);
      updateCart();
    }
    function checkout() {
      alert('Checkout not implemented.');
    }
    updateCart();
  </script>
</body>
</html>
```

Simple Checkout Form

```
<!DOCTYPE html>
<html lang="en">
<head>
  <meta charset="UTF-8">
  <meta name="viewport" content="width=device-width, initial-scale=1.0">
  <title>Checkout Form</title>
  <style>
    body { font-family: Arial, sans-serif; }
    form { width: 300px; margin: 50px auto; }
    label, input { display: block; width: 100%; margin-bottom: 10px; }
    input[type="submit"] { width: auto; }
  </style>
```

```
</head>
<body>
  <h1>Checkout Form</h1>
  <form id="checkoutForm" onsubmit="submitForm(event)">
    <label for="name">Name</label>
    <input type="text" id="name" name="name" required>
    <label for="address">Address</label>
    <input type="text" id="address" name="address" required>
    <label for="email">Email</label>
    <input type="email" id="email" name="email" required>
    <label for="card">Credit Card</label>
    <input type="text" id="card" name="card" required>
    <input type="submit" value="Submit">
  </form>
  <script>
    function submitForm(event) {
      event.preventDefault();
      const formData = new FormData(document.getElementById('checkoutForm'));
      const data = Object.fromEntries(formData.entries());
      console.log('Form Data Submitted:', data);
      alert('Checkout submitted successfully.');
    }
  </script>
</body>
</html>
```

8.FORM ENHANCEMENTS

Progress Indicator for Long Forms

```
<!DOCTYPE html>
<html lang="en">
<head>
  <meta charset="UTF-8">
  <meta name="viewport" content="width=device-width, initial-scale=1.0">
  <title>Form Progress Indicator</title>
  <style>
    body { font-family: Arial, sans-serif; }
    .form-section { display: none; }
    .form-section.active { display: block; }
    #progressBar { width: 100%; background-color: #f3f3f3; }
    #progress { width: 0%; height: 30px; background-color: #4caf50; }
    button { margin: 10px 0; }
  </style>
</head>
<body>
  <h1>Form with Progress Indicator</h1>
  <div id="progressBar">
    <div id="progress"></div>
  </div>
  <form id="longForm">
    <div class="form-section active">
      <h2>Section 1</h2>
      <label for="name">Name</label>
      <input type="text" id="name" name="name" required>
      <button type="button" onclick="nextSection()">Next</button>
    </div>
    <div class="form-section">
```

```
    <h2>Section 2</h2>
    <label for="email">Email</label>
    <input type="email" id="email" name="email" required>
    <button type="button" onclick="previousSection()">Previous</button>
    <button type="button" onclick="nextSection()">Next</button>
  </div>
  <div class="form-section">
    <h2>Section 3</h2>
    <label for="password">Password</label>
    <input type="password" id="password" name="password" required>
    <button type="button" onclick="previousSection()">Previous</button>
    <button type="submit">Submit</button>
  </div>
</form>
<script>
  const sections = document.querySelectorAll('.form-section');
  let currentSection = 0;

  function showSection(index) {
    sections.forEach((section, i) => {
      section.classList.toggle('active', i === index);
    });
    updateProgress(index);
  }

  function updateProgress(index) {
    const progress = document.getElementById('progress');
    const progressPercentage = ((index + 1) / sections.length) * 100;
    progress.style.width = progressPercentage + '%';
  }
```

```
    function nextSection() {
      if (currentSection < sections.length - 1) {
        currentSection++;
        showSection(currentSection);
      }
    }

    function previousSection() {
      if (currentSection > 0) {
        currentSection--;
        showSection(currentSection);
      }
    }

    document.getElementById('longForm').addEventListener('submit', (event) => {
      event.preventDefault();
      alert('Form submitted successfully!');
    });
  </script>
</body>
</html>
```

Password Strength Meter

```
<!DOCTYPE html>
<html lang="en">
<head>
  <meta charset="UTF-8">
  <meta name="viewport" content="width=device-width, initial-scale=1.0">
  <title>Password Strength Meter</title>
  <style>
```

```
    body { font-family: Arial, sans-serif; text-align: center; }
    #strengthMeter { width: 100%; height: 10px; background-color: #ddd; margin-top: 10px; }
    #strengthBar { height: 10px; width: 0; background-color: red; }
  </style>
</head>
<body>
  <h1>Password Strength Meter</h1>
  <form>
    <label for="password">Password</label>
    <input type="password" id="password" name="password" required>
    <div id="strengthMeter">
      <div id="strengthBar"></div>
    </div>
  </form>
  <script>
    const passwordInput = document.getElementById('password');
    const strengthBar = document.getElementById('strengthBar');
    passwordInput.addEventListener('input', () => {
      const strength = getPasswordStrength(passwordInput.value);
      strengthBar.style.width = strength + '%';
      if (strength < 50) {
        strengthBar.style.backgroundColor = 'red';
      } else if (strength < 80) {
        strengthBar.style.backgroundColor = 'orange';
      } else {
        strengthBar.style.backgroundColor = 'green';
      }
    });
    function getPasswordStrength(password) {
      let strength = 0;
```

```
      if (password.length >= 8) strength += 25;
      if (/[A-Z]/.test(password)) strength += 25;
      if (/[a-z]/.test(password)) strength += 25;
      if (/[0-9]/.test(password)) strength += 15;
      if (/[\W]/.test(password)) strength += 10;
      return strength;
    }
  </script>
</body>
</html>
```

Dynamic Dependent Dropdowns

```
<!DOCTYPE html>
<html lang="en">
<head>
  <meta charset="UTF-8">
  <meta name="viewport" content="width=device-width, initial-scale=1.0">
  <title>Dynamic Dependent Dropdowns</title>
  <style>
    body { font-family: Arial, sans-serif; text-align: center; }
  </style>
</head>
<body>
  <h1>Dynamic Dependent Dropdowns</h1>
  <form>
    <label for="country">Country</label>
    <select id="country" onchange="updateCities()">
      <option value="">Select Country</option>
      <option value="USA">USA</option>
      <option value="Canada">Canada</option>
    </select>
```

```
    <label for="city">City</label>
    <select id="city">
      <option value="">Select City</option>
    </select>
  </form>
  <script>
    const citiesByCountry = {
      USA: ['New York', 'Los Angeles', 'Chicago'],
      Canada: ['Toronto', 'Vancouver', 'Montreal']
    };
    function updateCities() {
      const countrySelect = document.getElementById('country');
      const citySelect = document.getElementById('city');
      const selectedCountry = countrySelect.value;
      citySelect.innerHTML = '<option value="">Select City</option>';
      if (selectedCountry && citiesByCountry[selectedCountry]) {
        citiesByCountry[selectedCountry].forEach(city => {
          const option = document.createElement('option');
          option.value = city;
          option.textContent = city;
          citySelect.appendChild(option);
        });
      }
    }
  </script>
</body>
</html>
```

9.ACCESSIBILITY

Screen Reader Compatibility Test

```
<!DOCTYPE html>
<html lang="en">
<head>
  <meta charset="UTF-8">
  <meta name="viewport" content="width=device-width, initial-scale=1.0">
  <title>Screen Reader Compatibility Test</title>
</head>
<body>
  <h1>Screen Reader Compatibility Test</h1>
  <p>This page is for testing screen reader compatibility.</p>
  <!-- Test Text -->
  <h2>Test Text</h2>
  <p>This is a sample paragraph for testing screen reader compatibility.</p>
  <!-- Test Links -->
  <h2>Test Links</h2>
  <ul>
    <li><a href="#">Link 1</a></li>
    <li><a href="#">Link 2</a></li>
    <li><a href="#">Link 3</a></li>
  </ul>
  <!-- Test Buttons -->
  <h2>Test Buttons</h2>
  <button onclick="alert('Button 1 clicked')">Button 1</button>
  <button onclick="alert('Button 2 clicked')">Button 2</button>
  <button onclick="alert('Button 3 clicked')">Button 3</button>

  <!-- Test Form -->
  <h2>Test Form</h2>
```

```
  <form>
    <label for="inputField">Input Field:</label>
    <input type="text" id="inputField" name="inputField">
    <br><br>
    <label for="checkbox">Checkbox:</label>
    <input type="checkbox" id="checkbox" name="checkbox">
    <br><br>
    <label for="radio1">Radio 1:</label>
    <input type="radio" id="radio1" name="radioGroup">
    <br>
    <label for="radio2">Radio 2:</label>
    <input type="radio" id="radio2" name="radioGroup">
    <br>
    <label for="radio3">Radio 3:</label>
    <input type="radio" id="radio3" name="radioGroup">
    <br><br>
    <button type="submit">Submit</button>
    <button type="reset">Reset</button>
  </form>
</body>
</html>
```

10.CUSTOMIZABLE LAYOUTS

Responsive Layout for Different Devices

```
<!DOCTYPE html>
<html lang="en">
<head>
  <meta charset="UTF-8">
  <meta name="viewport" content="width=device-width, initial-scale=1.0">
  <title>Responsive Layout</title>
  <style>
    body { font-family: Arial, sans-serif; }
    .container { width: 80%; margin: 0 auto; }
    .box { width: 100%; height: 100px; background-color: #f2f2f2; margin-bottom: 20px; }
    @media (min-width: 768px) {
      .container { width: 75%; }
    }
    @media (min-width: 992px) {
      .container { width: 70%; }
    }
    @media (min-width: 1200px) {
      .container { width: 65%; }
    }
  </style>
</head>
<body>
  <h1>Responsive Layout for Different Devices</h1>
  <div class="container">
    <div class="box"></div>
    <div class="box"></div>
    <div class="box"></div>
  </div>
```

```
</body>
</html>
```

Sticky Header/Footer

```
<!DOCTYPE html>
<html lang="en">
<head>
  <meta charset="UTF-8">
  <meta name="viewport" content="width=device-width, initial-scale=1.0">
  <title>Sticky Header/Footer</title>
  <style>
    body { font-family: Arial, sans-serif; margin: 0; padding: 0; }
    header { background-color: #333; color: #fff; padding: 20px 0; position: sticky; top: 0; width: 100%; z-index: 1000; }
    footer { background-color: #333; color: #fff; padding: 20px 0; position: sticky; bottom: 0; width: 100%; z-index: 1000; }
    .content { height: 2000px; padding: 20px; }
  </style>
</head>
<body>
  <header>
    <h1>Sticky Header</h1>
  </header>
  <div class="content">
    <h2>Content Goes Here</h2>
    <p>This is a sample content area. Scroll down to see the sticky footer.</p>
  </div>
  <footer>
    <h2>Sticky Footer</h2>
  </footer>
</body>
```

```
</html>
```

Image Grid with Masonry-like Layout

```
<!DOCTYPE html>
<html lang="en">
<head>
  <meta charset="UTF-8">
  <meta name="viewport" content="width=device-width, initial-scale=1.0">
  <title>Image Grid with Masonry-like Layout</title>
  <style>
    body { font-family: Arial, sans-serif; margin: 0; padding: 0; }
    .grid { column-count: 3; column-gap: 10px; }
    .grid-item { break-inside: avoid; margin-bottom: 10px; }
    img { max-width: 100%; height: auto; }
    @media (max-width: 768px) {
      .grid { column-count: 2; }
    }
    @media (max-width: 480px) {
      .grid { column-count: 1; }
    }
  </style>
</head>
<body>
  <h1>Image Grid with Masonry-like Layout</h1>
  <div class="grid">
    <div class="grid-item"><img src="image1.jpg" alt="Image 1"></div>
    <div class="grid-item"><img src="image2.jpg" alt="Image 2"></div>
    <div class="grid-item"><img src="image3.jpg" alt="Image 3"></div>
    <div class="grid-item"><img src="image4.jpg" alt="Image 4"></div>
    <div class="grid-item"><img src="image5.jpg" alt="Image 5"></div>
    <div class="grid-item"><img src="image6.jpg" alt="Image 6"></div>
```

```
  </div>
</body>
</html>
```

11.BASIC DRAWING AND GRAPHICS

Line Drawing Tool

```
<!DOCTYPE html>
<html lang="en">
<head>
  <meta charset="UTF-8">
  <meta name="viewport" content="width=device-width, initial-scale=1.0">
  <title>Line Drawing Tool</title>
  <style>
    body { font-family: Arial, sans-serif; }
    canvas { border: 1px solid #000; }
  </style>
</head>
<body>
  <h1>Line Drawing Tool</h1>
  <canvas id="canvas" width="800" height="400"></canvas>
  <script>
    const canvas = document.getElementById('canvas');
    const context = canvas.getContext('2d');
    let isDrawing = false;
    canvas.addEventListener('mousedown', startDrawing);
    canvas.addEventListener('mousemove', draw);
    canvas.addEventListener('mouseup', stopDrawing);
    canvas.addEventListener('mouseout', stopDrawing);
    function startDrawing(event) {
      isDrawing = true;
      context.beginPath();
      context.moveTo(event.clientX - canvas.offsetLeft, event.clientY - canvas.offsetTop);
    }
    function draw(event) {
```

```
      if (isDrawing) {
        context.lineTo(event.clientX - canvas.offsetLeft, event.clientY - canvas.offsetTop);
        context.stroke();
      }
    }
    function stopDrawing() {
      isDrawing = false;
    }
  </script>
</body>
</html>
```

Shape Drawing Tool (Square, Circle, etc.)

```
<!DOCTYPE html>
<html lang="en">
<head>
  <meta charset="UTF-8">
  <meta name="viewport" content="width=device-width, initial-scale=1.0">
  <title>Shape Drawing Tool</title>
  <style>
    body { font-family: Arial, sans-serif; }
    canvas { border: 1px solid #000; }
  </style>
</head>
<body>
  <h1>Shape Drawing Tool</h1>
  <canvas id="canvas" width="800" height="400"></canvas>
  <button onclick="drawRectangle()">Draw Rectangle</button>
  <button onclick="drawCircle()">Draw Circle</button>
  <script>
    const canvas = document.getElementById('canvas');
```

```
    const context = canvas.getContext('2d');
    function drawRectangle() {
      context.clearRect(0, 0, canvas.width, canvas.height);
      context.fillRect(50, 50, 200, 100);
    }
    function drawCircle() {
      context.clearRect(0, 0, canvas.width, canvas.height);
      context.beginPath();
      context.arc(150, 150, 50, 0, 2 * Math.PI);
      context.stroke();
    }
  </script>
</body>
</html>
```

Simple Paint Application

```
<!DOCTYPE html>
<html lang="en">
<head>
  <meta charset="UTF-8">
  <meta name="viewport" content="width=device-width, initial-scale=1.0">
  <title>Simple Paint Application</title>
  <style>
    body { font-family: Arial, sans-serif; }
    canvas { border: 1px solid #000; }
  </style>
</head>
<body>
  <h1>Simple Paint Application</h1>
  <canvas id="canvas" width="800" height="400"></canvas>
  <button onclick="setColor('black')">Black</button>
```

```
<button onclick="setColor('red')">Red</button>
<button onclick="setColor('green')">Green</button>
<button onclick="setColor('blue')">Blue</button>
<script>
  const canvas = document.getElementById('canvas');
  const context = canvas.getContext('2d');
  let isDrawing = false;
  let currentColor = 'black';
  canvas.addEventListener('mousedown', startDrawing);
  canvas.addEventListener('mousemove', draw);
  canvas.addEventListener('mouseup', stopDrawing);
  canvas.addEventListener('mouseout', stopDrawing);
  function startDrawing(event) {
    isDrawing = true;
    context.beginPath();
    context.moveTo(event.clientX - canvas.offsetLeft, event.clientY - canvas.offsetTop);
  }
  function draw(event) {
    if (isDrawing) {
      context.strokeStyle = currentColor;
      context.lineTo(event.clientX - canvas.offsetLeft, event.clientY - canvas.offsetTop);
      context.stroke();
    }
  }
  function stopDrawing() {
    isDrawing = false;
  }

  function setColor(color) {
    currentColor = color;
```

```
    }
  </script>
</body>
</html>
```

12.ANIMATIONS WITH USER INPUT

Mouse Hover Parallax Effect

```
<!DOCTYPE html>
<html lang="en">
<head>
  <meta charset="UTF-8">
  <meta name="viewport" content="width=device-width, initial-scale=1.0">
  <title>Mouse Hover Parallax Effect</title>
  <style>
    body { font-family: Arial, sans-serif; margin: 0; padding: 0; overflow-x: hidden; }
    .container { width: 100%; height: 100vh; overflow: hidden; position: relative; }
    .background { width: 100%; height: 100%; position: absolute; top: 0; left: 0; background:
url('background.jpg') center/cover no-repeat; }
    .foreground { position: absolute; top: 50%; left: 50%; transform: translate(-50%, -50%); }
    .text { font-size: 24px; color: #fff; }
  </style>
</head>
<body>
  <h1>Mouse Hover Parallax Effect</h1>
  <div class="container">
    <div class="background"></div>
    <div class="foreground">
      <p class="text">Move your mouse over the background to see the parallax effect.</p>
    </div>
  </div>
  <script>
    const foreground = document.querySelector('.foreground');
    const parallaxStrength = 20;
    document.addEventListener('mousemove', (event) => {
      const x = (window.innerWidth - event.pageX * parallaxStrength) / 100;
```

```
      const y = (window.innerHeight - event.pageY * parallaxStrength) / 100;
      foreground.style.transform = `translate(${x}px, ${y}px)`;
    });
  </script>
</body>
</html>
```

Click-to-Animate Elements Mouse Hover Parallax Effect

```
<!DOCTYPE html>
<html lang="en">
<head>
  <meta charset="UTF-8">
  <meta name="viewport" content="width=device-width, initial-scale=1.0">
  <title>Mouse Hover Parallax Effect</title>
  <style>
    body { font-family: Arial, sans-serif; margin: 0; padding: 0; overflow-x: hidden; }
    .container { width: 100%; height: 100vh; overflow: hidden; position: relative; }
    .background { width: 100%; height: 100%; position: absolute; top: 0; left: 0; background:
url('background.jpg') center/cover no-repeat; }
    .foreground { position: absolute; top: 50%; left: 50%; transform: translate(-50%, -50%); }
    .text { font-size: 24px; color: #fff; }
  </style>
</head>
<body>
  <h1>Mouse Hover Parallax Effect</h1>
  <div class="container">
    <div class="background"></div>
    <div class="foreground">
      <p class="text">Move your mouse over the background to see the parallax effect.</p>
    </div>
  </div>
```

```
  <script>
    const foreground = document.querySelector('.foreground');
    const parallaxStrength = 20;
    document.addEventListener('mousemove', (event) => {
      const x = (window.innerWidth - event.pageX * parallaxStrength) / 100;
      const y = (window.innerHeight - event.pageY * parallaxStrength) / 100;
      foreground.style.transform = `translate(${x}px, ${y}px)`;
    });
  </script>
</body>
</html>
```

Click-to-Animate Elements

```
<!DOCTYPE html>
<html lang="en">
<head>
  <meta charset="UTF-8">
  <meta name="viewport" content="width=device-width, initial-scale=1.0">
  <title>Click-to-Animate Elements</title>
  <style>
    body { font-family: Arial, sans-serif; margin: 0; padding: 0; }
    .box { width: 100px; height: 100px; background-color: #007bff; position: absolute; transition: transform 0.5s ease; }
  </style>
</head>
<body>
  <h1>Click-to-Animate Elements</h1>
  <div class="box" onclick="animateBox(this)"></div>
  <script>
    function animateBox(element) {
      const randomX = Math.floor(Math.random() * (window.innerWidth - 100));
```

```
      const randomY = Math.floor(Math.random() * (window.innerHeight - 100));
      element.style.transform = `translate(${randomX}px, ${randomY}px)`;
    }
  </script>
</body>
</html>
```

Interactive Drawing with User Input

```
<!DOCTYPE html>
<html lang="en">
<head>
  <meta charset="UTF-8">
  <meta name="viewport" content="width=device-width, initial-scale=1.0">
  <title>Interactive Drawing with User Input</title>
  <style>
    body { font-family: Arial, sans-serif; margin: 0; padding: 0; }
    canvas { border: 1px solid #000; }
  </style>
</head>
<body>
  <h1>Interactive Drawing with User Input</h1>
  <canvas id="canvas" width="800" height="400"></canvas>
  <input type="color" id="colorPicker">
  <input type="range" id="brushSize" min="1" max="50" value="10">

  <script>
    const canvas = document.getElementById('canvas');
    const context = canvas.getContext('2d');
    let isDrawing = false;

    canvas.addEventListener('mousedown', startDrawing);
```

```
    canvas.addEventListener('mousemove', draw);
    canvas.addEventListener('mouseup', stopDrawing);
    canvas.addEventListener('mouseout', stopDrawing);

    function startDrawing(event) {
      isDrawing = true;
      context.beginPath();
      context.moveTo(event.clientX - canvas.offsetLeft, event.clientY - canvas.offsetTop);
    }

    function draw(event) {
      if (isDrawing) {
        const color = document.getElementById('colorPicker').value;
        const brushSize = document.getElementById('brushSize').value;
        context.strokeStyle = color;
        context.lineWidth = brushSize;
        context.lineTo(event.clientX - canvas.offsetLeft, event.clientY - canvas.offsetTop);
        context.stroke();
      }
    }

    function stopDrawing() {
      isDrawing = false;
    }
  </script>
</body>
</html>
```

13.MORE GAMES

Rock-Paper-Scissors

```
<!DOCTYPE html>
<html lang="en">
<head>
  <meta charset="UTF-8">
  <meta name="viewport" content="width=device-width, initial-scale=1.0">
  <title>Rock-Paper-Scissors</title>
  <style>
    body { font-family: Arial, sans-serif; }
    .choices { display: flex; justify-content: center; margin-bottom: 20px; }
    .choices button { margin: 0 10px; padding: 10px 20px; font-size: 16px; }
    .result { text-align: center; font-size: 24px; }
  </style>
</head>
<body>
  <h1>Rock-Paper-Scissors</h1>
  <div class="choices">
    <button onclick="playGame('rock')">Rock</button>
    <button onclick="playGame('paper')">Paper</button>
    <button onclick="playGame('scissors')">Scissors</button>
  </div>
  <div class="result" id="result"></div>
  <script>
    function playGame(playerChoice) {
      const choices = ['rock', 'paper', 'scissors'];
      const computerChoice = choices[Math.floor(Math.random() * choices.length)];
      let result;
      if (playerChoice === computerChoice) {
        result = 'It\'s a tie!';
```

```
    } else if (
      (playerChoice === 'rock' && computerChoice === 'scissors') ||
      (playerChoice === 'paper' && computerChoice === 'rock') ||
      (playerChoice === 'scissors' && computerChoice === 'paper')
    ) {
      result = 'You win!';
    } else {
      result = 'Computer wins!';
    }
    document.getElementById('result').textContent = `Player chose ${playerChoice}, Computer chose ${computerChoice}. ${result}`;
   }
  </script>
</body>
</html>
```

Simon Says

```
<!DOCTYPE html>
<html lang="en">
<head>
  <meta charset="UTF-8">
  <meta name="viewport" content="width=device-width, initial-scale=1.0">
  <title>Simon Says</title>
  <style>
    body { font-family: Arial, sans-serif; text-align: center; }
    .button-container { margin-top: 20px; }
    button { margin: 10px; padding: 10px 20px; font-size: 16px; }
  </style>
</head>
<body>
  <h1>Simon Says</h1>
```

```
  <div id="sequence"></div>
  <div class="button-container">
    <button onclick="startGame()">Start Game</button>
    <button onclick="checkSequence()">Check Sequence</button>
  </div>
  <script>
    const colors = ['red', 'blue', 'green', 'yellow'];
    let sequence = [];
    function startGame() {
      sequence.push(colors[Math.floor(Math.random() * colors.length)]);
      displaySequence();
    }
    function displaySequence() {
      const sequenceElement = document.getElementById('sequence');
      sequenceElement.textContent = sequence.join(' ');
    }
    function checkSequence() {
      const input = prompt('Enter the sequence (separated by spaces):').trim().split(' ');
      if (input.join('') === sequence.join('')) {
        alert('Correct sequence! You win!');
      } else {
        alert('Incorrect sequence! Game over.');
        sequence = [];
      }
    }
  </script>
</body>
</html>
```

Word Search

```
<!DOCTYPE html>
<html lang="en">
<head>
  <meta charset="UTF-8">
  <meta name="viewport" content="width=device-width, initial-scale=1.0">
  <title>Word Search</title>
  <style>
    body { font-family: Arial, sans-serif; }
    .word-search { display: grid; gap: 2px; }
    .cell { width: 30px; height: 30px; background-color: #eee; border: 1px solid #ddd; text-align: center; font-size: 16px; }
  </style>
</head>
<body>
  <h1>Word Search</h1>
  <div class="word-search">
    <div class="row">
      <div class="cell">W</div>
      <div class="cell">O</div>
      <div class="cell">R</div>
      <div class="cell">D</div>
    </div>
    <div class="row">
      <div class="cell">S</div>
      <div class="cell">E</div>
      <div class="cell">A</div>
      <div class="cell">R</div>
    </div>
    <div class="row">
```

```
      <div class="cell">C</div>
      <div class="cell">H</div>
      <div class="cell"></div>
      <div class="cell"></div>
    </div>
    <div class="row">
      <div class="cell"></div>
      <div class="cell"></div>
      <div class="cell"></div>
      <div class="cell"></div>
    </div>
  </div>
</body>
</html>
```

Matching Game

```
<!DOCTYPE html>
<html lang="en">
<head>
  <meta charset="UTF-8">
  <meta name="viewport" content="width=device-width, initial-scale=1.0">
  <title>Matching Game</title>
  <style>
    body { font-family: Arial, sans-serif; }
    .game-container { display: flex; flex-wrap: wrap; width: 300px; }
    .card { width: 100px; height: 100px; background-color: #ccc; margin: 5px; display: flex;
justify-content: center; align-items: center; font-size: 24px; cursor: pointer; }
    .hidden { display: none; }
  </style>
</head>
<body>
```

```
<h1>Matching Game</h1>
<div class="game-container">
  <div class="card" onclick="revealCard(0)">A</div>
  <div class="card" onclick="revealCard(1)">B</div>
  <div class="card" onclick="revealCard(2)">C</div>
  <div class="card" onclick="revealCard(3)">D</div>
  <div class="card" onclick="revealCard(4)">A</div>
  <div class="card" onclick="revealCard(5)">B</div>
  <div class="card" onclick="revealCard(6)">C</div>
  <div class="card" onclick="revealCard(7)">D</div>
</div>

<script>
  let revealedCards = [];
  let matchedPairs = 0;

  function revealCard(index) {
    const card = document.querySelectorAll('.card')[index];
    card.classList.add('hidden');
    revealedCards.push({ index, value: card.textContent });

    if (revealedCards.length === 2) {
      setTimeout(checkMatch, 1000);
    }
  }

  function checkMatch() {
    const [firstCard, secondCard] = revealedCards;
    if (firstCard.value === secondCard.value) {
      document.querySelectorAll('.card')[firstCard.index].classList.add('hidden');
```

```
      document.querySelectorAll('.card')[secondCard.index].classList.add('hidden');
      matchedPairs++;
      if (matchedPairs === 4) {
       alert('Congratulations! You have matched all pairs!');
      }
     } else {
      document.querySelectorAll('.card')[firstCard.index].classList.remove('hidden');
      document.querySelectorAll('.card')[secondCard.index].classList.remove('hidden');
     }
     revealedCards = [];
    }
  </script>
</body>
</html>
```

14.DATA MANIPULATION

Simple Data Table with Sorting

```
<!DOCTYPE html>
<html lang="en">
<head>
  <meta charset="UTF-8">
  <meta name="viewport" content="width=device-width, initial-scale=1.0">
  <title>Simple Data Table with Sorting</title>
  <style>
    body { font-family: Arial, sans-serif; }
    table { border-collapse: collapse; width: 100%; }
    th, td { border: 1px solid #ddd; padding: 8px; text-align: left; }
    th { cursor: pointer; }
  </style>
</head>
<body>
  <h1>Simple Data Table with Sorting</h1>
  <table id="dataTable">
    <thead>
      <tr>
        <th onclick="sortTable(0)">ID</th>
        <th onclick="sortTable(1)">Name</th>
        <th onclick="sortTable(2)">Age</th>
      </tr>
    </thead>
    <tbody>
      <tr><td>1</td><td>John</td><td>25</td></tr>
      <tr><td>2</td><td>Alice</td><td>30</td></tr>
      <tr><td>3</td><td>Bob</td><td>28</td></tr>
    </tbody>
```

```
  </table>
  <script>
    function sortTable(columnIndex) {
      const table = document.getElementById('dataTable');
      const rows = Array.from(table.rows).slice(1);
      const sortOrder = table.rows[0].cells[columnIndex].getAttribute('data-order') || 'asc';
      rows.sort((a, b) => {
        const aValue = a.cells[columnIndex].textContent.trim();
        const bValue = b.cells[columnIndex].textContent.trim();
        return sortOrder === 'asc' ? aValue.localeCompare(bValue) :
bValue.localeCompare(aValue);
      });

      while (table.rows.length > 1) {
        table.deleteRow(1);
      }
      rows.forEach(row => {
        table.appendChild(row);
      });
      table.rows[0].cells[columnIndex].setAttribute('data-order', sortOrder === 'asc' ? 'desc' : 'asc');
    }
  </script>
</body>
</html>
```

Search Functionality on a Data Set

```
<!DOCTYPE html>
<html lang="en">
<head>
  <meta charset="UTF-8">
  <meta name="viewport" content="width=device-width, initial-scale=1.0">
```

```
  <title>Search Functionality on a Data Set</title>
  <style>
    body { font-family: Arial, sans-serif; }
    input { padding: 8px; font-size: 16px; margin-bottom: 10px; }
    table { border-collapse: collapse; width: 100%; }
    th, td { border: 1px solid #ddd; padding: 8px; text-align: left; }
  </style>
</head>
<body>
  <h1>Search Functionality on a Data Set</h1>
  <input type="text" id="searchInput" placeholder="Search...">
  <table id="dataTable">
    <thead>
      <tr>
        <th>ID</th>
        <th>Name</th>
        <th>Age</th>
      </tr>
    </thead>
    <tbody>
      <tr><td>1</td><td>John</td><td>25</td></tr>
      <tr><td>2</td><td>Alice</td><td>30</td></tr>
      <tr><td>3</td><td>Bob</td><td>28</td></tr>
    </tbody>
  </table>
  <script>
    document.getElementById('searchInput').addEventListener('keyup', function() {
      const searchValue = this.value.toLowerCase();
      const table = document.getElementById('dataTable');
      const rows = table.getElementsByTagName('tr');
```

```
    for (let i = 1; i < rows.length; i++) {
     const cells = rows[i].getElementsByTagName('td');
     let found = false;
     for (let j = 0; j < cells.length; j++) {
      const cellValue = cells[j].textContent.toLowerCase();
      if (cellValue.includes(searchValue)) {
       found = true;
       break;
      }
     }
     rows[i].style.display = found ? '' : 'none';
    }
   });
  </script>
</body>
</html>
```

15.MORE INTERACTIVE ELEMENTS

Progress Circle

```
<!DOCTYPE html>
<html lang="en">
<head>
  <meta charset="UTF-8">
  <meta name="viewport" content="width=device-width, initial-scale=1.0">
  <title>Progress Circle</title>
  <style>
    body { font-family: Arial, sans-serif; text-align: center; }
    .progress-circle { width: 100px; height: 100px; position: relative; }
    .progress-circle .progress-fill { position: absolute; left: 0; top: 0; width: 100%; height: 100%;
border-radius: 50%; background-color: #ccc; clip: rect(0, 50px, 100px, 0); }
    .progress-circle .progress-fill::after { content: ''; position: absolute; top: 0; left: 0; width:
100%; height: 100%; border-radius: 50%; background-color: #007bff; clip: rect(0, 100px, 100px,
50px); }
    .progress-circle .progress-text { position: absolute; top: 50%; left: 0; width: 100%; transform:
translateY(-50%); font-size: 24px; color: #000; }
  </style>
</head>
<body>
  <h1>Progress Circle</h1>
  <div class="progress-circle">
    <div class="progress-fill" style="transform: rotate(90deg);"></div>
    <div class="progress-text">75%</div>
  </div>
</body>
</html>
```

Social Sharing Buttons

```
<!DOCTYPE html>
<html lang="en">
<head>
  <meta charset="UTF-8">
  <meta name="viewport" content="width=device-width, initial-scale=1.0">
  <title>Social Sharing Buttons</title>
  <style>
    body { font-family: Arial, sans-serif; text-align: center; }
    .social-buttons { margin-top: 20px; }
    .social-buttons button { margin: 5px; padding: 10px 20px; font-size: 16px; }
  </style>
</head>
<body>
  <h1>Social Sharing Buttons</h1>
  <div class="social-buttons">
    <button onclick="shareOnFacebook()">Share on Facebook</button>
    <button onclick="shareOnTwitter()">Share on Twitter</button>
    <button onclick="shareOnLinkedIn()">Share on LinkedIn</button>
  </div>
  <script>
    function shareOnFacebook() {
      alert('Sharing on Facebook...');
    }
    function shareOnTwitter() {
      alert('Sharing on Twitter...');
    }
    function shareOnLinkedIn() {
      alert('Sharing on LinkedIn...');
    }
```

```
  </script>
</body>
</html>
```

Rating System with Stars

```
<!DOCTYPE html>
<html lang="en">
<head>
  <meta charset="UTF-8">
  <meta name="viewport" content="width=device-width, initial-scale=1.0">
  <title>Rating System with Stars</title>
  <style>
    body { font-family: Arial, sans-serif; text-align: center; }
    .stars { margin: 20px auto; }
    .star { font-size: 24px; color: #ccc; cursor: pointer; }
    .star:hover { color: #ffc107; }
    .star.checked { color: #ffc107; }
  </style>
</head>
<body>
  <h1>Rating System with Stars</h1>
  <div class="stars">
    <span class="star" onclick="rate(1)">★</span>
    <span class="star" onclick="rate(2)">★</span>
    <span class="star" onclick="rate(3)">★</span>
    <span class="star" onclick="rate(4)">★</span>
    <span class="star" onclick="rate(5)">★</span>
  </div>

  <script>
```

```
    function rate(stars) {
     const starElements = document.querySelectorAll('.star');
     for (let i = 0; i < starElements.length; i++) {
      if (i < stars) {
       starElements[i].classList.add('checked');
      } else {
       starElements[i].classList.remove('checked');
      }
     }
    }
  </script>
</body>
</html>
```

16.MORE USER INTERACTION

Text Highlighter

```
<!DOCTYPE html>
<html lang="en">
<head>
  <meta charset="UTF-8">
  <meta name="viewport" content="width=device-width, initial-scale=1.0">
  <title>Text Highlighter</title>
  <style>
    body { font-family: Arial, sans-serif; }
    .highlighted { background-color: yellow; }
  </style>
</head>
<body>
  <h1>Text Highlighter</h1>
  <p id="text">Lorem ipsum dolor sit amet, consectetur adipiscing elit. Sed ac dolor ac magna
sollicitudin feugiat.</p>
  <button onclick="highlightText()">Highlight Text</button>
  <script>
    function highlightText() {
      const text = document.getElementById('text');
      const wordsToHighlight = ['Lorem', 'dolor'];
           wordsToHighlight.forEach(word => {
        const regex = new RegExp(`\\b${word}\\b`, 'gi');
        const replacedText = text.innerHTML.replace(regex, `<span
class="highlighted">${word}</span>`);
        text.innerHTML = replacedText;
      });
    }
  </script>
```

```
</body>
</html>
```

Custom Cursors

```
<!DOCTYPE html>
<html lang="en">
<head>
  <meta charset="UTF-8">
  <meta name="viewport" content="width=device-width, initial-scale=1.0">
  <title>Custom Cursors</title>
  <style>
    body { font-family: Arial, sans-serif; cursor: url('custom-cursor.png'), auto; }
    .custom-cursor { position: absolute; width: 20px; height: 20px; background-color: red; border-radius: 50%; pointer-events: none; }
  </style>
</head>
<body>
  <h1>Custom Cursors</h1>
  <div class="custom-cursor"></div>
  <script>
    document.addEventListener('mousemove', function(event) {
      const customCursor = document.querySelector('.custom-cursor');
      customCursor.style.left = `${event.clientX}px`;
      customCursor.style.top = `${event.clientY}px`;
    });
  </script>
</body>
</html>
```

17.MORE ANIMATIONS

Text Typing Animation

```
<!DOCTYPE html>
<html lang="en">
<head>
  <meta charset="UTF-8">
  <meta name="viewport" content="width=device-width, initial-scale=1.0">
  <title>Text Typing Animation</title>
  <style>
    body { font-family: Arial, sans-serif; }
    #text { font-size: 24px; }
  </style>
</head>
<body>
  <h1>Text Typing Animation</h1>
  <p id="text"></p>

  <script>
    const textElement = document.getElementById('text');
    const text = "Lorem ipsum dolor sit amet, consectetur adipiscing elit. Sed ac dolor ac magna sollicitudin feugiat.";

    function typeText(index) {
      if (index < text.length) {
        textElement.textContent += text.charAt(index);
        setTimeout(() => {
          typeText(index + 1);
        }, 50); // Adjust typing speed here
      }
    }
```

```
    typeText(0);
  </script>
</body>
</html>
```

Element Bouncing Animation

```
<!DOCTYPE html>
<html lang="en">
<head>
  <meta charset="UTF-8">
  <meta name="viewport" content="width=device-width, initial-scale=1.0">
  <title>Element Bouncing Animation</title>
  <style>
    body { font-family: Arial, sans-serif; }
    .element { width: 100px; height: 100px; background-color: #007bff; position: absolute; top: 0; left: 0; animation: bounce 2s infinite alternate; }

    @keyframes bounce {
      from { top: 0; }
      to { top: 100px; }
    }
  </style>
</head>
<body>
  <h1>Element Bouncing Animation</h1>
  <div class="element"></div>
</body>
</html>
```

18.MORE DATA VISUALIZATION

Gauge Chart

```
<!DOCTYPE html>
<html lang="en">
<head>
  <meta charset="UTF-8">
  <meta name="viewport" content="width=device-width, initial-scale=1.0">
  <title>Gauge Chart</title>
  <script src="https://cdn.jsdelivr.net/npm/chart.js"></script>
</head>
<body>
  <h1>Gauge Chart</h1>
  <canvas id="gaugeChart" width="400" height="400"></canvas>
  <script>
    const ctx = document.getElementById('gaugeChart').getContext('2d');
    const gaugeChart = new Chart(ctx, {
      type: 'doughnut',
      data: {
        labels: ['Value', 'Remaining'],
        datasets: [{
          data: [75, 25],
          backgroundColor: ['#007bff', '#e0e0e0'],
          borderWidth: 0
        }]
      },
      options: {
        rotation: Math.PI,
        circumference: Math.PI,
        cutoutPercentage: 80,
        plugins: {
```

```
          datalabels: {
            display: false
          }
        }
      }
    });
  </script>
</body>
</html>
```

Scatter Plot

```
<!DOCTYPE html>
<html lang="en">
<head>
  <meta charset="UTF-8">
  <meta name="viewport" content="width=device-width, initial-scale=1.0">
  <title>Scatter Plot</title>
  <script src="https://cdn.jsdelivr.net/npm/chart.js"></script>
</head>
<body>
  <h1>Scatter Plot</h1>
  <canvas id="scatterPlot" width="400" height="400"></canvas>
  <script>
    const ctx = document.getElementById('scatterPlot').getContext('2d');
    const scatterPlot = new Chart(ctx, {
      type: 'scatter',
      data: {
        datasets: [{
          label: 'Scatter Dataset',
          data: [
            { x: -10, y: 0 },
```

```
          { x: 0, y: 10 },
          { x: 10, y: 5 },
          { x: 0.5, y: 5.5 }
        ],
        backgroundColor: '#007bff'
      }]
    },
    options: {
      scales: {
        x: {
          type: 'linear',
          position: 'bottom'
        }
      }
    }
  });
</script>
</body>
</html>
```

Animated Charts

```
<!DOCTYPE html>
<html lang="en">
<head>
  <meta charset="UTF-8">
  <meta name="viewport" content="width=device-width, initial-scale=1.0">
  <title>Animated Charts</title>
  <script src="https://cdn.jsdelivr.net/npm/chart.js"></script>
</head>
<body>
  <h1>Animated Charts</h1>
```

```
<canvas id="animatedChart" width="400" height="400"></canvas>
<script>
  const ctx = document.getElementById('animatedChart').getContext('2d');
  const animatedChart = new Chart(ctx, {
    type: 'bar',
    data: {
      labels: ['Red', 'Blue', 'Yellow', 'Green', 'Purple', 'Orange'],
      datasets: [{
        label: '# of Votes',
        data: [12, 19, 3, 5, 2, 3],
        backgroundColor: [
          'rgba(255, 99, 132, 0.2)',
          'rgba(54, 162, 235, 0.2)',
          'rgba(255, 206, 86, 0.2)',
          'rgba(75, 192, 192, 0.2)',
          'rgba(153, 102, 255, 0.2)',
          'rgba(255, 159, 64, 0.2)'
        ],
        borderColor: [
          'rgba(255, 99, 132, 1)',
          'rgba(54, 162, 235, 1)',
          'rgba(255, 206, 86, 1)',
          'rgba(75, 192, 192, 1)',
          'rgba(153, 102, 255, 1)',
          'rgba(255, 159, 64, 1)'
        ],
        borderWidth: 1
      }]
    },
    options: {
```

```
      animation: {
        duration: 2000,
        easing: 'easeInOutBounce'
      },
      scales: {
        y: {
          beginAtZero: true
        }
      }
    }
  });
 </script>
</body>
</html>
```

19.MORE GAMES

Snake Game

```
<!DOCTYPE html>
<html lang="en">
<head>
 <meta charset="UTF-8">
 <meta name="viewport" content="width=device-width, initial-scale=1.0">
 <title>Snake Game</title>
 <style>
  canvas { background-color: #000; display: block; margin: 0 auto; }
 </style>
</head>
<body>
 <h1 style="text-align: center;">Snake Game</h1>
 <canvas id="gameCanvas" width="400" height="400"></canvas>
 <script>
  const canvas = document.getElementById('gameCanvas');
  const ctx = canvas.getContext('2d');
  const box = 20;
  let snake = [{ x: 9 * box, y: 10 * box }];
  let direction = null;
  let food = {
   x: Math.floor(Math.random() * 19 + 1) * box,
   y: Math.floor(Math.random() * 19 + 1) * box
  };

  document.addEventListener('keydown', changeDirection);

  function changeDirection(event) {
   if (event.keyCode == 37 && direction != 'RIGHT') direction = 'LEFT';
```

```
    else if (event.keyCode == 38 && direction != 'DOWN') direction = 'UP';
    else if (event.keyCode == 39 && direction != 'LEFT') direction = 'RIGHT';
    else if (event.keyCode == 40 && direction != 'UP') direction = 'DOWN';
  }

  function draw() {
    ctx.clearRect(0, 0, canvas.width, canvas.height);
    for (let i = 0; i < snake.length; i++) {
      ctx.fillStyle = (i == 0) ? 'green' : 'white';
      ctx.fillRect(snake[i].x, snake[i].y, box, box);
    }
    ctx.fillStyle = 'red';
    ctx.fillRect(food.x, food.y, box, box);

    let snakeX = snake[0].x;
    let snakeY = snake[0].y;

    if (direction == 'LEFT') snakeX -= box;
    if (direction == 'UP') snakeY -= box;
    if (direction == 'RIGHT') snakeX += box;
    if (direction == 'DOWN') snakeY += box;

    if (snakeX == food.x && snakeY == food.y) {
      food = {
        x: Math.floor(Math.random() * 19 + 1) * box,
        y: Math.floor(Math.random() * 19 + 1) * box
      };
    } else {
      snake.pop();
    }
```

```
      let newHead = { x: snakeX, y: snakeY };
      if (snakeX < 0 || snakeY < 0 || snakeX >= canvas.width || snakeY >= canvas.height ||
collision(newHead, snake)) {
        clearInterval(game);
      }
      snake.unshift(newHead);
    }

    function collision(head, array) {
      for (let i = 0; i < array.length; i++) {
        if (head.x == array[i].x && head.y == array[i].y) {
          return true;
        }
      }
      return false;
    }

    let game = setInterval(draw, 100);
  </script>
</body>
</html>
```

Breakout Game

```
<!DOCTYPE html>
<html lang="en">
<head>
  <meta charset="UTF-8">
  <meta name="viewport" content="width=device-width, initial-scale=1.0">
  <title>Breakout Game</title>
  <style>
```

```
    canvas { background: #eee; display: block; margin: 0 auto; }
  </style>
</head>
<body>
  <h1 style="text-align: center;">Breakout Game</h1>
  <canvas id="breakoutCanvas" width="480" height="320"></canvas>

  <script>
    const canvas = document.getElementById('breakoutCanvas');
    const ctx = canvas.getContext('2d');
    const ballRadius = 10;
    let x = canvas.width / 2;
    let y = canvas.height - 30;
    let dx = 2;
    let dy = -2;
    const paddleHeight = 10;
    const paddleWidth = 75;
    let paddleX = (canvas.width - paddleWidth) / 2;
    let rightPressed = false;
    let leftPressed = false;
    const brickRowCount = 5;
    const brickColumnCount = 3;
    const brickWidth = 75;
    const brickHeight = 20;
    const brickPadding = 10;
    const brickOffsetTop = 30;
    const brickOffsetLeft = 30;
    let bricks = [];
    for (let c = 0; c < brickColumnCount; c++) {
      bricks[c] = [];
```

```
    for (let r = 0; r < brickRowCount; r++) {
      bricks[c][r] = { x: 0, y: 0, status: 1 };
    }
  }

  document.addEventListener('keydown', keyDownHandler, false);
  document.addEventListener('keyup', keyUpHandler, false);

  function keyDownHandler(e) {
    if (e.key == 'Right' || e.key == 'ArrowRight') {
      rightPressed = true;
    } else if (e.key == 'Left' || e.key == 'ArrowLeft') {
      leftPressed = true;
    }
  }

  function keyUpHandler(e) {
    if (e.key == 'Right' || e.key == 'ArrowRight') {
      rightPressed = false;
    } else if (e.key == 'Left' || e.key == 'ArrowLeft') {
      leftPressed = false;
    }
  }

  function collisionDetection() {
    for (let c = 0; c < brickColumnCount; c++) {
      for (let r = 0; r < brickRowCount; r++) {
        let b = bricks[c][r];
        if (b.status == 1) {
          if (x > b.x && x < b.x + brickWidth && y > b.y && y < b.y + brickHeight) {
```

```
          dy = -dy;
          b.status = 0;
        }
      }
    }
  }
}

function drawBall() {
  ctx.beginPath();
  ctx.arc(x, y, ballRadius, 0, Math.PI * 2);
  ctx.fillStyle = '#0095DD';
  ctx.fill();
  ctx.closePath();
}

function drawPaddle() {
  ctx.beginPath();
  ctx.rect(paddleX, canvas.height - paddleHeight, paddleWidth, paddleHeight);
  ctx.fillStyle = '#0095DD';
  ctx.fill();
  ctx.closePath();
}

function drawBricks() {
  for (let c = 0; c < brickColumnCount; c++) {
    for (let r = 0; r < brickRowCount; r++) {
      if (bricks[c][r].status == 1) {
        let brickX = c * (brickWidth + brickPadding) + brickOffsetLeft;
        let brickY = r * (brickHeight + brickPadding) + brickOffsetTop;
```

```
        bricks[c][r].x = brickX;
        bricks[c][r].y = brickY;
        ctx.beginPath();
        ctx.rect(brickX, brickY, brickWidth, brickHeight);
        ctx.fillStyle = '#0095DD';
        ctx.fill();
        ctx.closePath();
      }
    }
  }
}

function draw() {
  ctx.clearRect(0, 0, canvas.width, canvas.height);
  drawBricks();
  drawBall();
  drawPaddle();
  collisionDetection();

  if (x + dx > canvas.width - ballRadius || x + dx < ballRadius) {
    dx = -dx;
  }
  if (y + dy < ballRadius) {
    dy = -dy;
  } else if (y + dy > canvas.height - ballRadius) {
    if (x > paddleX && x < paddleX + paddleWidth) {
      dy = -dy;
    } else {
      document.location.reload();
    }
```

```
    }

    if (rightPressed && paddleX < canvas.width - paddleWidth) {
      paddleX += 7;
    } else if (leftPressed && paddleX > 0) {
      paddleX -= 7;
    }

    x += dx;
    y += dy;
    requestAnimationFrame(draw);
  }

  draw();
 </script>
</body>
</html>
```

Maze Generator

```
<!DOCTYPE html>
<html lang="en">
<head>
 <meta charset="UTF-8">
 <meta name="viewport" content="width=device-width, initial-scale=1.0">
 <title>Maze Generator</title>
 <style>
  canvas { background: #eee; display: block; margin: 0 auto; }
 </style>
</head>
<body>
 <h1 style="text-align: center;">Maze Generator</h1>
```

```
<canvas id="mazeCanvas" width="400" height="400"></canvas>

<script>
  const canvas = document.getElementById('mazeCanvas');
  const ctx = canvas.getContext('2d');
  const cols = 20;
  const rows = 20;
  const cellSize = canvas.width / cols;
  const grid = [];
  let current;
  const stack = [];

  class Cell {
    constructor(x, y) {
      this.x = x;
      this.y = y;
      this.walls = [true, true, true, true];
      this.visited = false;
    }

    show() {
      const x = this.x * cellSize;
      const y = this.y * cellSize;
      ctx.strokeStyle = '#000';
      ctx.lineWidth = 2;

      if (this.walls[0]) ctx.strokeRect(x, y, cellSize, 0);          // Top
      if (this.walls[1]) ctx.strokeRect(x + cellSize, y, 0, cellSize); // Right
      if (this.walls[2]) ctx.strokeRect(x, y + cellSize, cellSize, 0); // Bottom
      if (this.walls[3]) ctx.strokeRect(x, y, 0, cellSize);          // Left
```

```
      if (this.visited) {
        ctx.fillStyle = '#fff';
        ctx.fillRect(x, y, cellSize, cellSize);
      }
    }

    checkNeighbors() {
      const neighbors = [];
      const top = grid[index(this.x, this.y - 1)];
      const right = grid[index(this.x + 1, this.y)];
      const bottom = grid[index(this.x, this.y + 1)];
      const left = grid[index(this.x - 1, this.y)];

      if (top && !top.visited) neighbors.push(top);
      if (right && !right.visited) neighbors.push(right);
      if (bottom && !bottom.visited) neighbors.push(bottom);
      if (left && !left.visited) neighbors.push(left);

      if (neighbors.length > 0) {
        const r = Math.floor(Math.random() * neighbors.length);
        return neighbors[r];
      } else {
        return undefined;
      }
    }
  }

  function index(x, y) {
    if (x < 0 || y < 0 || x >= cols || y >= rows) {
```

```
    return -1;
   }
  return x + y * cols;
 }

 function setup() {
  for (let y = 0; y < rows; y++) {
   for (let x = 0; x < cols; x++) {
    const cell = new Cell(x, y);
    grid.push(cell);
   }
  }
  current = grid[0];
 }

 function draw() {
  ctx.clearRect(0, 0, canvas.width, canvas.height);
  grid.forEach(cell => cell.show());

  current.visited = true;
  const next = current.checkNeighbors();
  if (next) {
   next.visited = true;
   stack.push(current);
   removeWalls(current, next);
   current = next;
  } else if (stack.length > 0) {
   current = stack.pop();
  }
```

```
    requestAnimationFrame(draw);
  }

  function removeWalls(a, b) {
    const x = a.x - b.x;
    if (x === 1) {
      a.walls[3] = false;
      b.walls[1] = false;
    } else if (x === -1) {
      a.walls[1] = false;
      b.walls[3] = false;
    }

    const y = a.y - b.y;
    if (y === 1) {
      a.walls[0] = false;
      b.walls[2] = false;
    } else if (y === -1) {
      a.walls[2] = false;
      b.walls[0] = false;
    }
  }

  setup();
  draw();
 </script>
</body>
</html>
```

20.MORE APPLICATIONS

Simple Music Player

```
<!DOCTYPE html>
<html lang="en">
<head>
  <meta charset="UTF-8">
  <meta name="viewport" content="width=device-width, initial-scale=1.0">
  <title>Simple Music Player</title>
  <style>
    body { font-family: Arial, sans-serif; text-align: center; }
    audio { margin-top: 20px; }
  </style>
</head>
<body>
  <h1>Simple Music Player</h1>
  <audio controls>
    <source src="your-music-file.mp3" type="audio/mp3">
    Your browser does not support the audio element.
  </audio>
</body>
</html>
```

Quote Generator

```
<!DOCTYPE html>
<html lang="en">
<head>
  <meta charset="UTF-8">
  <meta name="viewport" content="width=device-width, initial-scale=1.0">
  <title>Quote Generator</title>
  <style>
    body { font-family: Arial, sans-serif; text-align: center; margin-top: 50px; }
```

```
    button { margin-top: 20px; padding: 10px 20px; }
    p { font-size: 24px; }
  </style>
</head>
<body>
  <h1>Quote Generator</h1>
  <p id="quote">Click the button to generate a quote!</p>
  <button onclick="generateQuote()">New Quote</button>

  <script>
    const quotes = [
      "The best way to predict the future is to create it.",
      "Life is 10% what happens to us and 90% how we react to it.",
      "The only way to do great work is to love what you do.",
      "The only limit to our realization of tomorrow is our doubts of today."
    ];

    function generateQuote() {
      const randomIndex = Math.floor(Math.random() * quotes.length);
      document.getElementById('quote').textContent = quotes[randomIndex];
    }
  </script>
</body>
</html>
```

Random Password Generator

```
<!DOCTYPE html>
<html lang="en">
<head>
  <meta charset="UTF-8">
  <meta name="viewport" content="width=device-width, initial-scale=1.0">
```

```
  <title>Random Password Generator</title>
  <style>
    body { font-family: Arial, sans-serif; text-align: center; margin-top: 50px; }
    button { margin-top: 20px; padding: 10px 20px; }
    input { font-size: 24px; text-align: center; }
  </style>
</head>
<body>
  <h1>Random Password Generator</h1>
  <input type="text" id="password" readonly>
  <br>
  <button onclick="generatePassword()">Generate Password</button>

  <script>
    function generatePassword() {
      const characters =
'ABCDEFGHIJKLMNOPQRSTUVWXYZabcdefghijklmnopqrstuvwxyz0123456789!@#$%^&
*()';
      const passwordLength = 12;
      let password = '';
      for (let i = 0; i < passwordLength; i++) {
        const randomIndex = Math.floor(Math.random() * characters.length);
        password += characters[randomIndex];
      }
      document.getElementById('password').value = password;
    }
  </script>
</body>
</html>
```

21.BEYOND THE BASICS

Drag and Drop Sorting List

```
<!DOCTYPE html>
<html lang="en">
<head>
  <meta charset="UTF-8">
  <meta name="viewport" content="width=device-width, initial-scale=1.0">
  <title>Drag and Drop Sorting List</title>
  <style>
    ul { list-style-type: none; padding: 0; width: 200px; }
    li { padding: 10px; border: 1px solid #ccc; margin-bottom: 5px; background: #f9f9f9; cursor:
move; }
  </style>
</head>
<body>
  <h1>Drag and Drop Sorting List</h1>
  <ul id="sortable">
    <li draggable="true">Item 1</li>
    <li draggable="true">Item 2</li>
    <li draggable="true">Item 3</li>
    <li draggable="true">Item 4</li>
  </ul>
  <script>
    const sortable = document.getElementById('sortable');
    let draggingEle;
    let placeholder;
    let isDraggingStarted = false;

    const swap = (nodeA, nodeB) => {
      const parentA = nodeA.parentNode;
```

```
    const siblingA = nodeA.nextSibling === nodeB ? nodeA : nodeA.nextSibling;
    nodeB.parentNode.insertBefore(nodeA, nodeB);
    parentA.insertBefore(nodeB, siblingA);
  };

  const mouseMoveHandler = function (e) {
    const draggingRect = draggingEle.getBoundingClientRect();
    if (!isDraggingStarted) {
      isDraggingStarted = true;
      placeholder = document.createElement('div');
      placeholder.classList.add('placeholder');
      draggingEle.parentNode.insertBefore(placeholder, draggingEle.nextSibling);
      placeholder.style.height = `${draggingRect.height}px`;
    }

    draggingEle.style.position = 'absolute';
    draggingEle.style.top = `${e.clientY - draggingRect.height / 2}px`;
    draggingEle.style.left = `${e.clientX - draggingRect.width / 2}px`;

    const prevEle = draggingEle.previousElementSibling;
    const nextEle = placeholder.nextElementSibling;

    if (prevEle && isAbove(draggingEle, prevEle)) {
      swap(placeholder, draggingEle);
      swap(placeholder, prevEle);
      return;
    }

    if (nextEle && isAbove(nextEle, draggingEle)) {
      swap(nextEle, placeholder);
```

```
      swap(nextEle, draggingEle);
    }
  };

  const isAbove = (nodeA, nodeB) => {
    const rectA = nodeA.getBoundingClientRect();
    const rectB = nodeB.getBoundingClientRect();

    return (rectA.top + rectA.height / 2) < (rectB.top + rectB.height / 2);
  };

  const mouseUpHandler = function () {
    placeholder && placeholder.parentNode.removeChild(placeholder);
    draggingEle.style.removeProperty('top');
    draggingEle.style.removeProperty('left');
    draggingEle.style.removeProperty('position');
    draggingEle = null;
    isDraggingStarted = false;

    document.removeEventListener('mousemove', mouseMoveHandler);
    document.removeEventListener('mouseup', mouseUpHandler);
  };

  const mouseDownHandler = function (e) {
    draggingEle = e.target;
    const rect = draggingEle.getBoundingClientRect();
    document.addEventListener('mousemove', mouseMoveHandler);
    document.addEventListener('mouseup', mouseUpHandler);
  };
```

```
    sortable.querySelectorAll('li').forEach(function (item) {
      item.addEventListener('mousedown', mouseDownHandler);
    });
  </script>
</body>
</html>
```

Image Preloader (displays a placeholder while image loads)

```
<!DOCTYPE html>
<html lang="en">
<head>
  <meta charset="UTF-8">
  <meta name="viewport" content="width=device-width, initial-scale=1.0">
  <title>Image Preloader</title>
  <style>
    .image-container {
      position: relative;
      width: 300px;
      height: 300px;
      background: #f0f0f0;
    }
    .image-container img {
      display: none;
      width: 100%;
      height: 100%;
    }
    .loader {
      position: absolute;
      top: 50%;
      left: 50%;
      transform: translate(-50%, -50%);
```

```
      border: 16px solid #f3f3f3;
      border-radius: 50%;
      border-top: 16px solid #3498db;
      width: 120px;
      height: 120px;
      animation: spin 2s linear infinite;
    }
    @keyframes spin {
      0% { transform: rotate(0deg); }
      100% { transform: rotate(360deg); }
    }
  </style>
</head>
<body>
  <h1>Image Preloader</h1>
  <div class="image-container">
    <div class="loader"></div>
    <img src="your-image.jpg" alt="Preloaded Image" onload="imageLoaded(this)">
  </div>

  <script>
    function imageLoaded(img) {
      img.style.display = 'block';
      img.previousElementSibling.style.display = 'none';
    }
  </script>
</body>
</html>
```

Lazy Loading (loads content only when scrolled into view)

```
<!DOCTYPE html>
<html lang="en">
<head>
  <meta charset="UTF-8">
  <meta name="viewport" content="width=device-width, initial-scale=1.0">
  <title>Lazy Loading</title>
  <style>
    .lazy-load {
      min-height: 300px;
      background: #eee;
      margin: 20px 0;
    }
  </style>
</head>
<body>
  <h1>Lazy Loading</h1>
  <div class="lazy-load" data-src="your-image.jpg">Loading...</div>
  <div class="lazy-load" data-src="your-image2.jpg">Loading...</div>
  <div class="lazy-load" data-src="your-image3.jpg">Loading...</div>

  <script>
    document.addEventListener('DOMContentLoaded', function () {
      const lazyLoadElements = document.querySelectorAll('.lazy-load');
      const config = {
        rootMargin: '0px 0px 50px 0px',
        threshold: 0.01
      };

      let observer = new IntersectionObserver(function (entries, self) {
```

```
        entries.forEach(entry => {
          if (entry.isIntersecting) {
            const lazyElement = entry.target;
            const src = lazyElement.getAttribute('data-src');
            lazyElement.style.backgroundImage = `url(${src})`;
            lazyElement.textContent = '';
            self.unobserve(lazyElement);
          }
        });
      }, config);

      lazyLoadElements.forEach(lazyElement => {
        observer.observe(lazyElement);
      });
    });
  </script>
</body>
</html>
```

Cookie Consent Banner

```
<!DOCTYPE html>
<html lang="en">
<head>
  <meta charset="UTF-8">
  <meta name="viewport" content="width=device-width, initial-scale=1.0">
  <title>Cookie Consent Banner</title>
  <style>
    #cookieConsent {
      position: fixed;
      bottom: 0;
      left: 0;
```

```
      width: 100%;
      background: #000;
      color: #fff;
      padding: 10px;
      text-align: center;
      display: none;
    }
    #cookieConsent button {
      background: #f1d600;
      border: none;
      padding: 10px 20px;
      margin-left: 20px;
      cursor: pointer;
    }
  </style>
</head>
<body>
  <h1>Cookie Consent Banner</h1>
  <div id="cookieConsent">
    This website uses cookies to ensure you get the best experience. <button
onclick="acceptCookies()">Got it!</button>
  </div>

  <script>
    document.addEventListener('DOMContentLoaded', function () {
      if (!getCookie('acceptedCookies')) {
        document.getElementById('cookieConsent').style.display = 'block';
      }
    });
```

```
    function acceptCookies() {
      setCookie('acceptedCookies', 'true', 365);
      document.getElementById('cookieConsent').style.display = 'none';
    }

    function setCookie(name, value, days) {
      const d = new Date();
      d.setTime(d.getTime() + (days * 24 * 60 * 60 * 1000));
      const expires = "expires=" + d.toUTCString();
      document.cookie = name + "=" + value + ";" + expires + ";path=/";
    }

    function getCookie(name) {
      const cname = name + "=";
      const decodedCookie = decodeURIComponent(document.cookie);
      const ca = decodedCookie.split(';');
      for (let i = 0; i < ca.length; i++) {
        let c = ca[i];
        while (c.charAt(0) == ' ') {
          c = c.substring(1);
        }
        if (c.indexOf(cname) == 0) {
          return c.substring(cname.length, c.length);
        }
      }
      return "";
    }
  </script>
</body>
</html>
```

22.ACCESSIBILITY ENHANCEMENTS

Keyboard Navigation for Interactive Elements

```
<!DOCTYPE html>
<html lang="en">
<head>
  <meta charset="UTF-8">
  <meta name="viewport" content="width=device-width, initial-scale=1.0">
  <title>Keyboard Navigation for Interactive Elements</title>
  <style>
    .interactive {
      margin: 10px;
      padding: 10px;
      border: 1px solid #ccc;
    }
    .interactive:focus {
      outline: 2px solid #000;
      background: #f0f0f0;
    }
  </style>
</head>
<body>
  <h1>Keyboard Navigation for Interactive Elements</h1>
  <div tabindex="0" class="interactive" onclick="alert('Clicked Item 1')">Item 1</div>
  <div tabindex="0" class="interactive" onclick="alert('Clicked Item 2')">Item 2</div>
  <div tabindex="0" class="interactive" onclick="alert('Clicked Item 3')">Item 3</div>

  <script>
    document.addEventListener('keydown', function(e) {
      const activeElement = document.activeElement;
      if (e.key === 'Enter' && activeElement.classList.contains('interactive')) {
```

```
        activeElement.click();
      }
    });
  </script>
</body>
</html>
```

Screen Reader Text Alternatives for Images

```
<!DOCTYPE html>
<html lang="en">
<head>
  <meta charset="UTF-8">
  <meta name="viewport" content="width=device-width, initial-scale=1.0">
  <title>Screen Reader Text Alternatives for Images</title>
  <style>
    .image-container {
      position: relative;
      width: 300px;
    }
    .image-container img {
      width: 100%;
    }
    .sr-only {
      position: absolute;
      width: 1px;
      height: 1px;
      padding: 0;
      margin: -1px;
      overflow: hidden;
      clip: rect(0, 0, 0, 0);
      border: 0;
```

```
    }
  </style>
</head>
<body>
  <h1>Screen Reader Text Alternatives for Images</h1>
  <div class="image-container">
    <img src="your-image.jpg" alt="A description of the image">
    <span class="sr-only">A description of the image for screen readers</span>
  </div>
</body>
</html>
```

23.ADVANCED LAYOUTS

Multi-column Layout

```
<!DOCTYPE html>
<html lang="en">
<head>
  <meta charset="UTF-8">
  <meta name="viewport" content="width=device-width, initial-scale=1.0">
  <title>Multi-column Layout</title>
  <style>
    .multi-column {
      column-count: 3;
      column-gap: 20px;
    }
    .multi-column p {
      margin: 0 0 20px;
    }
  </style>
</head>
<body>
  <h1>Multi-column Layout</h1>
  <div class="multi-column">
    <p>Lorem ipsum dolor sit amet, consectetur adipiscing elit. Integer nec odio. Praesent libero.
Sed cursus ante dapibus diam.</p>
    <p>Sed nisi. Nulla quis sem at nibh elementum imperdiet. Duis sagittis ipsum. Praesent
mauris.</p>
    <p>Fusce nec tellus sed augue semper porta. Mauris massa. Vestibulum lacinia arcu eget
nulla.</p>
    <p>Class aptent taciti sociosqu ad litora torquent per conubia nostra, per inceptos himenaeos.
Curabitur sodales ligula in libero.</p>
  </div>
```

```
</body>
</html>
```

Grid-based Layout with Flexbox

```
<!DOCTYPE html>
<html lang="en">
<head>
  <meta charset="UTF-8">
  <meta name="viewport" content="width=device-width, initial-scale=1.0">
  <title>Grid-based Layout with Flexbox</title>
  <style>
    .flex-grid {
      display: flex;
      flex-wrap: wrap;
      gap: 20px;
    }
    .flex-grid > div {
      flex: 1 1 calc(33.333% - 20px);
      box-sizing: border-box;
      background: #f0f0f0;
      padding: 20px;
      text-align: center;
    }
  </style>
</head>
<body>
  <h1>Grid-based Layout with Flexbox</h1>
  <div class="flex-grid">
    <div>Item 1</div>
    <div>Item 2</div>
    <div>Item 3</div>
```

```
    <div>Item 4</div>
    <div>Item 5</div>
    <div>Item 6</div>
  </div>
</body>
</html>
```

Sticky Sidebar

```
<!DOCTYPE html>
<html lang="en">
<head>
  <meta charset="UTF-8">
  <meta name="viewport" content="width=device-width, initial-scale=1.0">
  <title>Sticky Sidebar</title>
  <style>
    .container {
      display: flex;
    }
    .main {
      flex: 1;
      padding: 20px;
    }
    .sidebar {
      width: 200px;
      padding: 20px;
      background: #f0f0f0;
      position: -webkit-sticky; /* Safari */
      position: sticky;
      top: 0;
    }
  </style>
```

```
</head>
<body>
  <h1>Sticky Sidebar</h1>
  <div class="container">
    <div class="main">
      <p>Lorem ipsum dolor sit amet, consectetur adipiscing elit. Integer nec odio. Praesent libero. Sed cursus ante dapibus diam. Sed nisi. Nulla quis sem at nibh elementum imperdiet. Duis sagittis ipsum. Praesent mauris.</p>
      <p>Fusce nec tellus sed augue semper porta. Mauris massa. Vestibulum lacinia arcu eget nulla. Class aptent taciti sociosqu ad litora torquent per conubia nostra, per inceptos himenaeos.</p>
      <p>Curabitur sodales ligula in libero. Sed dignissim lacinia nunc. Curabitur tortor. Pellentesque nibh. Aenean quam. In scelerisque sem at dolor.</p>
      <p>Maecenas mattis. Sed convallis tristique sem. Proin ut ligula vel nunc egestas porttitor. Morbi lectus risus, iaculis vel, suscipit quis, luctus non, massa.</p>
    </div>
    <div class="sidebar">
      Sticky Sidebar
    </div>
  </div>
</body>
</html>
```

24.ADVANCED ANIMATIONS

CSS3 Transitions and Animations

```
<!DOCTYPE html>
<html lang="en">
<head>
 <meta charset="UTF-8">
 <meta name="viewport" content="width=device-width, initial-scale=1.0">
 <title>CSS3 Transitions and Animations</title>
 <style>
  .box {
   width: 100px;
   height: 100px;
   background: #3498db;
   transition: transform 0.5s, background 0.5s;
   margin: 50px auto;
  }
  .box:hover {
   transform: rotate(45deg);
   background: #e74c3c;
  }
  .animated-box {
   width: 100px;
   height: 100px;
   background: #2ecc71;
   margin: 50px auto;
   animation: move 2s infinite alternate;
  }
  @keyframes move {
   0% {
    transform: translateX(0);
```

```
      }
      100% {
        transform: translateX(200px);
      }
    }
  </style>
</head>
<body>
  <h1>CSS3 Transitions and Animations</h1>
  <div class="box"></div>
  <div class="animated-box"></div>
</body>
</html>
```

SVG Animations

```
<!DOCTYPE html>
<html lang="en">
<head>
  <meta charset="UTF-8">
  <meta name="viewport" content="width=device-width, initial-scale=1.0">
  <title>SVG Animations</title>
  <style>
    svg {
      display: block;
      margin: 50px auto;
    }
  </style>
</head>
<body>
  <h1>SVG Animations</h1>
  <svg width="100" height="100" viewBox="0 0 100 100">
```

```
    <circle cx="50" cy="50" r="40" stroke="#3498db" stroke-width="4" fill="none">
      <animate attributeName="r" from="40" to="10" dur="1s" repeatCount="indefinite" />
      <animate attributeName="stroke" from="#3498db" to="#e74c3c" dur="1s"
repeatCount="indefinite" />
    </circle>
  </svg>
</body>
</html>
```

25.ADVANCED DATA VISUALIZATION

Interactive Charts with Libraries

```
<!DOCTYPE html>
<html lang="en">
<head>
  <meta charset="UTF-8">
  <meta name="viewport" content="width=device-width, initial-scale=1.0">
  <title>Interactive Charts with D3.js</title>
  <!-- Include D3.js library -->
  <script src="https://d3js.org/d3.v7.min.js"></script>
  <style>
    svg {
      width: 100%;
      height: 300px;
      background: #f0f0f0;
    }
  </style>
</head>
<body>
  <h1>Interactive Charts with D3.js</h1>
  <svg id="chart"></svg>

  <script>
    // Sample data
    const data = [30, 50, 70, 90, 110];

    // Set up SVG element
    const svg = d3.select('#chart');

    // Create bars
```

```
  svg.selectAll('rect')
   .data(data)
   .enter()
   .append('rect')
   .attr('x', (d, i) => i * 30)
   .attr('y', d => 300 - d)
   .attr('width', 25)
   .attr('height', d => d)
   .attr('fill', 'steelblue')
   .on('mouseover', function () {
    d3.select(this).attr('fill', 'orange');
   })
   .on('mouseout', function () {
    d3.select(this).attr('fill', 'steelblue');
   });
 </script>
</body>
</html>
```

Real-time Data Streaming

```
<!DOCTYPE html>
<html lang="en">
<head>
 <meta charset="UTF-8">
 <meta name="viewport" content="width=device-width, initial-scale=1.0">
 <title>Real-time Data Streaming</title>
 <style>
  #data-container {
   width: 100%;
   height: 300px;
   background: #f0f0f0;
```

```
      overflow: auto;
    }
  </style>
</head>
<body>
  <h1>Real-time Data Streaming</h1>
  <div id="data-container"></div>

  <script>
    // Simulating real-time data streaming
    setInterval(function() {
      const data = Math.random();
      const timestamp = new Date().toLocaleTimeString();
      const container = document.getElementById('data-container');
      const newData = `<p>${timestamp} - ${data}</p>`;
      container.insertAdjacentHTML('beforeend', newData);
      container.scrollTop = container.scrollHeight;
    }, 1000);
  </script>
</body>
</html>
```

www.ingramcontent.com/pod-product-compliance
Lightning Source LLC
Chambersburg PA
CBHW062139160726
48282CB00027B/881
* 9 7 8 9 3 3 4 0 7 4 2 0 8 *